The
Two-Body
Problem

PUBLISHING FOR THE WORLD
125 Years
THE JOHNS HOPKINS UNIVERSITY PRESS

The Two-Body Problem

Dual-Career-Couple Hiring Policies in Higher Education

LISA WOLF-WENDEL

SUSAN B. TWOMBLY

SUZANNE RICE

The Johns Hopkins
University Press
Baltimore & London

© 2003 The Johns Hopkins University Press
All rights reserved. Published 2003
Printed in the United States of America on acid-free paper

9 8 7 6 5 4 3 2 1

The Johns Hopkins University Press
2715 North Charles Street
Baltimore, Maryland 21218-4363
www.press.jhu.edu

Library of Congress Cataloging-in-Publication Data
Wolf-Wendel, Lisa.
   The two-body problem : dual-career-couple hiring policies in higher
education / Lisa Wolf-Wendel, Susan B. Twombly, Suzanne Rice.
       p.   cm.
Includes bibliographical references and index.
   ISBN 0-8018-7451-3 (hardcover : alk. paper)
   1. Academic couples—Employment—United States. 2. Academic
couples—Selection and appointment—United States. 3. Dual-career
families—Employment—United States. 4. Dual-career families—
Selection and appointment—United States. I. Twombly, Susan B.
II. Rice, Suzanne. III. Title.
   LB1778.45.W65 2004
   378.1'2—dc21

                                    2003006244

A catalog record for this book is available from the British Library.

CONTENTS

The
Two-Body
Problem

1 | Introduction

Two-body problem: As one body orbits the other, it tugs gravitationally on its partner, altering the original orbit. Then the second body does the same. In the end, there's this give-and-take of a dance, as each body influences the other, constantly changing its path. The bigger, more massive body moves the least, spending most of the time in the center of this dance. The smaller body has to careen all over the place, trying to find the right place to fit into the co-orbit.

What do Graham Spanier, president of Pennsylvania State University; Nan Keohane, president of Duke University; Ruth Atchley, assistant professor at the University of Kansas; Lucia Perillo, assistant professor at Southern Illinois University; Theodore Bromund, untenured instructor at Yale; and the fictitious Joshua Gordon, doctoral candidate, have in common?* The answer is that each is part of an academic couple in which one spouse or partner either is a tenure-track faculty member or is seeking such a position. Whether at the beginning of their careers, like Ruth Atchley and Joshua Gordon; in the middle, like Theodore Bromund and Lucia Perillo; or at the pinnacle, like Graham Spanier and Nan Keohane, each couple has experienced, and will continue to experience, the two-body problem. When searching for a job or deciding whether to accept an offer, one partner has to consider the career options for the other. For the particular couples mentioned here, some searches have ended happily and successfully, with both partners in tenure-track positions, if not in the same college or university, then close by. Others have found themselves commuting long distances or making compromises about the types of jobs they are willing to consider.

This book explores how colleges and universities have responded to the needs of dual-career academic couples, focusing on institutional policy and practice. Ultimately we seek to inform administrators and policymakers attempting to craft effective policies to meet the needs of dual-career couples.

The epigraph is from Michelle Thaller, February 25, 2002, www.csmonitor.com/atcsmonitor/cybercoverage/thaller/p-051701thallerdual.html.

*The names of these individuals have appeared in various articles about dual-career couples in the *Chronicle of Higher Education* during the past several years.

We do not intend to imply that the policies and practices we discuss can or should serve as models for all types of institutions to follow: nor are we implying that these policies and practices represent an exhaustive list of the options available. Rather, we hope to suggest alternatives for institutions to consider, given their own contexts and needs, as they grapple with the problem of dual-career couples. To a lesser extent, the book may provide useful information to couples who face the daunting challenge of finding two academic positions close together. At the end of this chapter we talk about meanings of various terms such as "spouse" and "partner," but it is important to note at the outset that we examine accommodation polices and practices for unmarried partners (same-sex and heterosexual) as well as for spouses.

An examination of the dual-career policies and practices within academe is important in large part because the experiences of the six people mentioned above are hardly unique. They are part of a fast growing number of academic couples in which both seek tenure-track faculty positions. One survey reported that 80 percent of faculty members had spouses or partners who were working professionals (Didion 1996). Increasingly, these spouses or partners are also academics. Astin and Milem (1997) reported that 35 percent of male faculty and 40 percent of female faculty nationally are partnered with other scholars who are faculty members.

Faculty couples have probably existed since women began to teach in higher education. Among the more famous cases was Alice Freeman Palmer. When she was appointed dean of women at the University of Chicago, she insisted she be required to work on site only twelve weeks out of the year because her husband, George Herbert Palmer, was a professor at Harvard (Nidiffer 2001). In *Women Scientists in America: Struggles and Strategies to 1940*, Rossiter (1982) includes a list of forty-nine notable couples in science before 1940. These couples include such famous academics as Margaret Mead and Gregory Bateson. In the late nineteenth century Ellen Swallow Richards and her husband, Robert Richards, were both on the faculty at MIT. While not all the couples on Rossiter's list comprised two faculty members, a good number did. Even less well known were single-sex female academic partnerships, which Palmieri (1995) describes as "Wellesley marriages" and which were found at many women's colleges in the late nineteenth century. Although the women Palmieri describes and many on Rossiter's list were anomalies in their day, the number of married or partnered academics has increased in recent years along with the number of women with Ph.D.s who are seeking faculty positions. Although women faculty are somewhat more likely to be single than men are (15 percent compared with 8 percent), married women faculty are more likely than men to be partnered with other academics (Astin and Milem 1997).

According to Astin and Milem (1997), the phenomenon of partnered academics varies considerably across the disciplines. For instance, women in the sciences are more likely than women in other fields to be married to academics. One study found that 80 percent of female mathematicians and 69 percent of women physicists are married to other scientists (McNeil and Sher 1998). Dual-career academic couples are so prevalent in the sciences that the "two-body problem" has become a common nickname for this situation. As even more women earn doctorates and attempt to join the faculty ranks in other disciplines as well as in the sciences, the number of dual-career couples in academia is expected to increase (Astin and Milem 1997; Burke 1988; Ferber and Loeb 1997).

Fifteen years ago, Burke (1988) concluded from her study of the academic labor market at research universities that "the spouse employment issue [is] now much more pronounced than it was in the 1950s" (78). Burke continues, "Spouse employment was a factor in almost 20 percent of the appointments and resignations" (78). It is safe to say that the "spouse employment issue" is now even more significant that it was in 1988. In all likelihood, the growing number of dual-career academic couples will challenge academic institutions' ability to recruit and retain faculty members (Bird and Bird 1987; Gee 1991; Preissler 1989; Smart and Smart 1990). For both men and women academics who are part of a dual-career couple, the decision to take a job, especially if the position requires relocation, brings the need for accommodation to the fore. In the past, their dual-career concerns were regarded as a burden to be shouldered by the couples themselves, especially when the academic labor market favored the hiring institution. When the faculty labor market was such that there were large numbers of Ph.D. holders clamoring for a relative handful of academic positions, institutions simply did not have to concern themselves with the needs of their faculties' spouses or partners.

Today, because of retirements and intense competition for the best faculty, the burden has begun to shift—at least partially—to institutions to help dual-career couples find suitable employment for their spouses and partners. Experts are projecting that the academic labor market will expand still further as senior faculty members retire (Finkelstein, Seal, and Schuster

1998). While it is likely that some of these openings will not be filled by ten-ure-track faculty (a significant problem for the future, but one beyond the scope of this book), many fields stand to benefit from this expansion of the academic labor market (Bowen and Sosa 1989; Finkelstein, Seal, and Schuster 1998). If academic institutions are to be competitive in filling their faculty openings with the best and brightest, they must be responsive to the needs of those seeking academic positions in ways they would not have been when there were more qualified applicants than jobs (Gee 1991).

Recent research and commentary about academic life clearly suggest that academic institutions have a lot to gain by paying attention to the needs of dual-career couples. If these needs are not addressed, they could translate into problems with faculty retention—a prospect with serious financial im-plications for colleges and universities (Boice 1992). Conversely, accommo-dating academic couples may well translate into improved retention when, for example, a faculty couple chooses to keep their academic positions rather than leave for an opportunity that pays better for one but offers the other less secure employment or none. Aside from aiding in recruitment and retention, there is also evidence that accommodating dual-career academic couples may boost research productivity. Specifically, the recent research literature suggests that being married to an academic is typically associated with greater productivity for academics than being single or being married to a nonacademic. These results hold true for both men and women (Astin and Davis 1985; Astin and Milem 1997; Bellas 1992; Bellas and Toutkoushian 1999; Long 1990; Ward and Grant 1996). These studies of faculty productivity center on publications, since publication is regarded as the primary indica-tor of faculty success (Jarvis 1992). It seems intuitive that dual-career assis-tance would enhance productivity in other areas of job responsibility as well (teaching, for example), but there is no empirical research that supports this contention.

The Larger Social Context for Dual-Career Couples

The literature on dual-career trends in other work sectors offers a few help-ful comparisons with the concerns and solutions for dual-career academic couples. Dual-career couples represent a growing trend in all work sectors. According to data from the U.S. Census and the Current Population Survey, in the year 2000 dual-earner married couples (families in which both husband and wife work) represented 37 percent of all families in the United States. Single men and women make up 25 percent of the employment sector, and single parents now represent close to 16 percent of working households. Further, "traditional" families, in which only the husband is employed, constitute only 19 percent of all families in the United States. These figures are unprecedented and reflect continuing growth and change over time. By way of comparison, dual-earner married couples constituted 8 percent of the population in 1920, 20 percent in 1950, and 38 percent in 1980. The decline since 1980 is best explained by the growth in single-parent households, which have increased from 11 percent in 1980 to 16 percent in 2000 (as cited by the Center for Work and Family Balance 2002).

According to research on dual-career couples by Phyllis Moen, director of the Cornell Employment and Family Careers Institute, 59 percent of men and 52 percent of women said that their spouses' careers were as important as their own (Moen et al. 1999). She also concludes that 39 percent of women and 12 percent of men consider their spouses' jobs to be *more* important than their own. Moen's research supports the idea that dual-career couples take into consideration the availability of employment opportunities for their spouses or partners when deciding where to work. In a study of dual-career couples in which both members had a college education, researchers found that these "power couples" were highly concentrated in large metropolitan areas. The researchers concluded that the returns to power couples of living in a large city rather than a small one have grown over time, in large part because large metropolitan areas tend to offer both members a greater variety of job opportunities (Costa and Kahn 1999).

In an environment in which dual-career couples are so prevalent, it should come as no surprise that most employment sectors are actively concerned about how to recruit and retain the best employees. When asked to anticipate the most important employment concern relating to relocation, 87 percent of human resource directors in business cited one partner's reluctance to give up a career, 83 percent cited the increase in dual careers, and 70 percent cited dependence on two incomes (Windham/NFTC 1995). Certainly most small companies do not have the resources to actively and formally help the accompanying spouse or partner in a dual-career couple find work. Large corporations, however, have actively engaged in providing their employees with relocation services, especially when recruiting more senior executives. The literature particularly notes that the prevalence of dual-career marriages is making it more difficult for multinational companies to relocate employees overseas (Organization Resources Counselors, Inc. 1998; Windham/NFTC 1995).

Many couples are unwilling to relocate unless the accompanying spouse or partner receives suitable employment assistance. As we discuss in more detail in chapter 4, these realities have led many large corporations to provide a host of relocation services, including helping spouses or partners find suitable work. Even the United States military recognizes that it must be responsive to the needs of dual-career couples—where both husband and wife are in the military and where only one spouse is. In 1988 the Department of Defense issued a directive that pertains to the employment and volunteer work of spouses of military personnel. According to the directive, the military must not "impede or otherwise interfere with the right of a spouse of a military member to pursue and hold a job . . . on or off a military installation." Further, the directive indicates that dual-career married couples are to be sent to the same geographic area whenever possible (Department of Defense 1988). In some cases the military has even outsourced a relocation program, using the same practices followed by the corporate sector to assist families in transition to a new community. This assistance includes helping spouses find employment (Lucas 1998).

What is most important to understand is that many larger employment sectors such as multinational corporations and the military recognize that dual-career couples are a development that must be addressed if they are to retain and recruit the best employees. There are, however, factors that make academic dual-career couples unique and perhaps more challenging to accommodate than couples in other work sectors. Unlike other professions such as medicine, law, elementary and high-school teaching, accounting, and real estate that can be practiced almost anywhere if one attains the appropriate state license, the training received by most people with academic doctorates is so specialized that suitable employment opportunities are very few. One cannot easily practice microbiology or philosophy, for example, outside a college or university. While in some fields the skills learned by those with a doctorate may be used in other settings, the training one receives as an academic can have very limited uses outside the academy. Adding to the difficulty, faculty positions are less concentrated in major metropolitan areas than other jobs requiring advanced education. While many large, prestigious higher education institutions are in major northeastern and West Coast metropolitan areas, many others are in relatively remote rural areas or in smaller towns and cities from the South to the Midwest. With the exception of relocation assistance services, which can be used in a variety of employment sectors including higher education, the realities of academic life and academic training make the search for solutions to the dual-career dilemma unique within higher education. As such, the solutions colleges and universities seek are for the most part unique to this employment sector.

Policy Studies Pertaining to Higher Education and Dual-Career Couples

Over the past several years much has been written about the trials, tribulations, and successes of dual-career academics from the perspective of individual faculty members and couples. In fact, over twenty stories about dual-career couples have appeared in the *Chronicle of Higher Education* during that period. The Big Ten universities even held a conference devoted to relocation for university employees, focusing particularly on faculty concerns. However, there is little in the literature that serves as a guide to institutions as they seek to find their way through rather complicated terrain.

Despite the increasing importance of dual-career couples as a policy concern for colleges and universities, no comprehensive national studies have systematically examined institutional policies and practices relating to dual-career couples in academe. What exists at present is a handful of smaller-scale studies suggesting that institutions are beginning to implement hiring policies for dual-career couples or have at least grappled with how to meet their needs. For example, Raabe (1997) conducted a national survey of academic vice presidents to determine the presence of a number of work and family supportive policies. Her research focused on various "family friendly" provisions, ranging from maternity and paternity leave to elder care, and including employment assistance for spouses. Raabe found that 44 percent of institutions provided some form of job assistance for spouses. An additional 12 percent were planning to implement such a policy. She concluded that research universities are the institutional type most likely to have a dual-career policy, in large part because they have more resources and more flexibility in creating positions, both academic and administrative, than do smaller institutions. However, she stopped short of exploring the specific kinds of policies being implemented or reporting on the consequences, motivations, or barriers to creating these policies. Indeed, only an unpublished study by Snyder (1990, cited in Loeb 1997), based on a survey of provosts at sixteen universities in Virginia, explores the way institutions assist spouses seeking faculty positions. This study concludes that at all of these institutions, at least some effort was made to find a faculty position for an accompanying spouse, though most of the efforts were ad hoc.

An analysis of the accommodation policy at the University of Illinois at Urbana-Champaign, provides some important insights into how that one institution has addressed the employment needs of dual-career academic couples (Loeb 1997). Illinois's practice of hiring dual-career academic couples began in the early 1980s as an ad hoc approach to recruiting desirable faculty members. According to Loeb's evaluation, between 1980 and 1994 ninety accommodations took place (Loeb 1997). Of those accommodated, the "primary hire" was more likely (77 percent) to be male. Loeb's data also indicate that the practice of accommodating spouses at Illinois increased dramatically since the early 1980s, with more than half of the couples who were accommodated receiving assistance between 1990 and 1994. And during this later period, cases where women were the primary hire rose to 29 percent. Of the accommodations made at Illinois during the study period, very few were within the same academic unit; most involved the cooperation of two departments, often in different colleges within the university. Loeb reports that some academic units (the social and behavioral sciences, the fields of law and veterinary medicine, agriculture, and education) are much more likely than others to engage in dual-career hiring. This is consistent with Astin and Milem's (1997) study, which also finds that dual-career academic couples are more likely to work in these fields. Further, Loeb reports that while the accommodated partner is more likely to hold a less desirable academic position than the "primary hire," most of this difference can be explained in terms of the relative strength of their credentials. Loeb found no evidence that any accompanying spouse was given a position for which he or she was unqualified merely because of the status of the "primary hire." Loeb concludes that the dual-career accommodation policy at Illinois is a success in that it has helped the institution recruit and retain faculty it otherwise might have lost.

Because of their size and limited resources, small colleges have less freedom to employ an accompanying spouse or partner of an initial hire. Several factors compound the situation for them. The first problem is that many academic couples both have their degrees in the same discipline (Miller-Loessi and Henderson 1997; Hogan 1998). This presents a problem for academic departments at small colleges, which may have only a handful of faculty positions. The situation is compounded in that many small colleges are in relatively small towns in rural areas with few other academic institutions within driving distance. The need to accommodate dual-career academic couples, however, is proportionally no less at small colleges. Hogan, in her 1998 survey of liberal arts colleges, found that 10 percent of the total faculty at her institutions of study were members of dual-career faculty couples. In fact, in our survey of Association of American Colleges and Universities (AAC&U) member institutions, liberal arts colleges were second only to research universities in their rating of the importance of responding to the needs of dual-career couples. In this book we report on two ways that small colleges attempt to meet the needs of dual-career academic couples: by creating shared or split positions and by sharing advertising with colleges in the same geographic region.

To provide some context, here are some recent data from the only study we know focused solely on dual-career hiring at liberal arts colleges (Hogan 1998). Hogan reports that between 1993 and 1998, the chief academic officers of selective liberal arts colleges reported hiring a total of 1,728 faculty members into tenure-track positions. Of these, 10 percent or 176 were members of couples in which both partners were academics. The percentage of faculty in dual academic partnerships was consistent across the five years. Because liberal arts colleges in larger towns (population 10,000 to 49,999) hired more faculty members than those in smaller towns, 37 percent or 66 of the dual-career faculty found themselves in larger towns. Another 37 percent were in smaller towns, while only 18 percent or 31 couples found themselves in cities over 50,000.

A fairly high number, 65 (37 percent), of the accompanying spouses or partners in Hogan's study reported being employed in a teaching capacity by the same institutions that hired their spouses. Half of these, or 32, were hired into full-time teaching positions, another 19 were employed part time, and 14 were hired into teaching positions that they shared with their partners (often called shared or split appointments) (Hogan 1998). Of those employed full time as faculty, very few were in tenure-track positions. Most of the appointments of accompanying spouses or partners in part-time and non-tenure-track full-time positions at these small colleges were happenstance (an opening was available when the demand presented itself) or the result of an ad hoc accommodation.

Each of the studies described provides an important base from which to engage in a more extensive examination of how colleges and universities attempt to provide for the employment needs of dual-career couples.

Overview

This book examines the policies and practices employed by colleges and universities that try to respond to the needs of dual-career couples, focusing specifically on cases where the initial hire is a faculty member as opposed to an administrator. We address such questions as, How prevalent are spouse and partner hiring policies? Who are institutions most likely to assist? What are the goals underlying the formation of a policy? How are institutions assisting spouses or partners? What are the strengths, weaknesses, and barriers to various approaches to accommodating couples? We use the perspectives of administrators and of faculty and their spouses and partners to describe the benefits, barriers, and unintended consequences institutions have encountered. We view these questions as important given the relative scarcity of policy-related research on dual-career couple accommodations and also their importance to recruitment, retention, and equity.

To answer these questions we have combined several research strategies to gather a range of data on dual-career couples in academia, including a survey of provosts, telephone interviews with fifteen deans of small colleges, a review of the literature on the topic, and in-depth case studies of several institutions that accommodate dual-career couples in different ways. By taking this approach we hope to illustrate the range of strategies currently being used by institutions trying to address the problem of dual-career couples and to suggest options for those considering how to approach the topic on their own campuses. The accommodation models are not intended as recipes or blueprints for institutions to follow, but they at least suggest the kinds of accommodations that seem to work relatively well given particular institutional features. In this regard, the book constitutes something of a practical guide. However, we go beyond the merely practical to discuss in depth some of the more perplexing and complicated issues arising from dual-career academic couples and attempts to accommodate them. Although we began the studies this book is based on almost wholeheartedly believing that accommodation policies are both positive and necessary, we have come to have a much more ambivalent view of dual-career hiring and the strategies used to make it happen. We thus point out the limitations of some purported "solutions" to the two-body problem, and we tackle some of the thorny issues frequently raised by opponents of spouse and partner accommodations. Aside from whatever practical guidance the book may provide, we hope that it will also shed some light on the arguments both for and against attempts at accommodation.

In chapter 2 we present the results of a survey sent to a national sample of chief academic officers whose universities are members of the AAC&U. This survey assessed the range of institutional policies and practices used to address spouse and partner employment needs. We report on the following:

- the types of institutions (e.g., four-year liberal arts, research 1) that have dual-career policies or practices;
- the characteristics of the faculty members institutions are most likely to assist;
- the number of faculty requests for assistance and types of assistance requested;
- institutions' reasons for accommodating or not accommodating spouses and partners;
- the nature of assistance given to faculty in dual-career couples;
- the perceived barriers to creating and implementing a dual-career policy.

Chapter 3 introduces the five case study sites we selected to represent a more in-depth view of the range of institutional responses to the hiring of dual-career couples. The chapter briefly describes the institutional characteristics of the case study sites and provides an overview of the accommodation they offer and a summary of the methods used to collect the data. We use pseudonyms to refer to the sites.

The next five chapters (chapters 4 through 8) are based on the in-depth case studies introduced in chapter 3. The chapters are organized according to the type of assistance offered, using reviews of relevant literature, policies found on the Internet and elsewhere as they relate to the specific type of assistance under consideration, and data from our case study sites. Drawing on information from the various sources, we describe why the institutions that take a specific approach do so and how they implement these approaches. Each of these chapters concludes with a discussion of the relative advantages and disadvantages of each approach.

More specifically, chapter 4 focuses on institutions that offer relocation services. Though fairly common in other employment sectors such as business, the military, and the foreign service, relocation services are relatively rare in higher education. These services are designed to help couples who are new to a community find their way around unfamiliar surroundings and to help the accompanying partner identify career opportunities within or outside the university. Two of the universities we studied devoted considerable resources to helping spouses and partners find nonfaculty positions either within or outside the university. Focusing on relocation services at "Heartland University" and "Riverdale University" as a base, we explore the different types and the various components of relocation services, how they work, and how such services benefit the university and those assisted. Although we did not originally intend to focus on services primarily devoted to helping spouses or partners adjust to the community or find employment off campus, we conclude that relocation services can be extremely beneficial, for a variety of reasons, and that all large universities should consider using them in some form to help couples make the transition to the new institution.

Chapter 5 describes the strategy of hiring an accompanying spouse or partner for a non-tenure-track or adjunct faculty position. This approach is the most common form of accommodation. All the case study sites we visited used this strategy, some in more formal ways than others. We highlight the Faculty Fellows Program at Heartland University and the less formal approach adopted at places like "Belle State." Heartland's policy is somewhat unusual because it provides a formal structure for employing spouses or partners in one-year appointments, paid for by the central administration. In contrast, Belle State takes the much more common approach of dealing with spouses or partners case by case and has no systematic, university-sponsored program for making such accommodations. We use these cases to highlight how these policies and strategies work and their strengths and weaknesses.

In chapter 6 we address shared positions as a means to accommodate dual-career academic couples. The chapter highlights how "Wildwood," a small liberal arts college in the Midwest, uses shared positions. The chapter discusses the extent and nature of shared positions and explores their benefits and limitations.

Chapter 7 focuses on a strategy especially suited to smaller colleges or universities: joint advertising among institutions that are within commuting distance of each other. Specifically, we describe several cooperative agreements between nearby academic institutions to jointly advertise academic positions in outlets such as the *Chronicle of Higher Education*. This shared advertising lets dual-career couples know when there may be employment for partners and spouses in nearby communities. Although joint advertising is a solution uniquely suited to institutions in relatively isolated regions of the country that are constrained by resources or size, it might be appropriate for other colleges and universities as well.

At least in the minds of many academic couples, securing two tenure-track positions at the same institution is the ultimate goal. Although the most sought-after, this kind of accommodation is clearly the most difficult to find. Most times when both partners find tenure-track employment at the same institution, it is the result of luck, being in the right place at the right time, and patience. This kind of accommodation is rare indeed; very few institutions are willing to create new faculty positions for spouses and partners, and very few couples are accommodated in this way. Chapter 8 describes in detail two universities that allow for creating such tenure-track positions— Riverdale and Hilltop. Each, however, takes a somewhat different approach. This chapter describes these approaches and discusses the strengths and weaknesses of each.

Attempts to accommodate dual-career faculty couples are not without controversy and problems. In fact, all opportunity hires, of which spouses or partners are one type, have come under considerable criticism (Wilson 2001). Chapter 9 outlines several common problems that may arise, focusing primarily on the concerns raised by hiring the accompanying spouse or partner at the university. While policies and practices to accommodate dual-career couples are generally positive for those accommodated, they raise interesting questions for the institutions making the accommodation. In this chapter we consider the fairness and legality of such policies; questions about how dual-career accommodations affect the quality of the faculty; the potential gap between the needs of a couple and the needs of a department; and how such policies affect faculty autonomy in hiring.

Chapter 10 summarizes the conclusions from our studies and the extant literature and makes recommendations for institutions regarding creating and implementing dual-career policies and strategies.

A Comment on Language

In *Through the Looking-Glass* (Carroll 1930), Humpty Dumpty exclaims, "When I use a word . . . it means just what I choose it to mean—neither more nor less." Of course, no one can make words mean exactly what they want; language just doesn't work that way. While there is always some slippage between what is written (or spoken) and what is read (or heard), in this book we use several words that seem especially likely to communicate meanings other than what we intend.

Let's start with the word "problem." We use the word in the title of this book not to imply that the growing presence of dual-career academic couples is necessarily undesirable. Rather, we conceptualize "problem" in Dewey's sense (1916). As Dewey understood it, a problem arises whenever we encounter a situation that is sufficiently novel that our established ways of thinking and acting prove inadequate. Thus a problem, for Dewey, is a challenge, an opportunity for growth—not something to be lamented. Indeed, Dewey famously claimed that "all genuine thinking begins with a problem." In an unchanging world, there would be no problems; but there would also be no opportunities for "genuine thought" or planned change. We see dual-career couples as a problem in this sense. More than ever before, the academic labor market now comprises a significant number of dual-career couples. Established approaches to personnel in higher education seem inadequate to respond to the needs of this new market.

In the literature on dual couples in academia, one finds numerous references to "leading" and "trailing" (or alternatively "primary" and "secondary") spouses and partners. We have tried to avoid these terms whenever possible. Intentionally or not, they imply a hierarchy of value that is bound to stigmatize faculty occupying the lower rung on this two-tiered ladder. Instead of using these more conventional terms, we refer to the "initial" and "accompanying" members of dual-career couples. While our alternative is less starkly hierarchical than, say, "leading" and "trailing," we are not entirely comfortable with it. After all, a common synonym for "initial" is "first." And to "accompany" is to go along with, while an accompanist is one who plays second fiddle to the main musical event. The fact of the matter is, however, that in most cases when an institution hires both members of a couple, this is because one member was initially offered a tenure-track position. Employment of the spouse or partner is contingent on the initial job offering, and we needed some way to refer to this aspect of dual-career hiring. We regret that we were unable to find language that avoids all unwarranted stigmatizing.

The word "accommodation" is generally used in a way that implies that when an institution hires both members of a couple it has compromised for their convenience. Indeed, the first definition of "accommodation" in our dictionary reads, "something supplied for convenience or to satisfy a need." The first definition of the verb "accommodate" reads, "to make fit, suitable, or congruous." To put the matter bluntly, the term suggests that colleges and universities that hire academic couples are kindly and yielding hosts to rather demanding (faculty) guests. But as we hope this book makes clear, one might just as reasonably mean by "accommodation" that a spouse or partner has compromised or at least modified his or her career goals in order to meet the employment needs not only of a partner but also of a college or university. In any event, "accommodation" in higher education is not, as common usage suggests, a unidirectional effort by institutions. So while we use the term "accommodation," we are mindful that this is much more of a two-way street than is generally implied.

Throughout most of this book, we refer to "spouses and partners." This rather awkward construction reflects two aspects of dual-career hiring in colleges and universities. First, the situation is so new that relatively few institutions have yet thought out whether they would hire both spouses and other domestic partners or just one or the other. Second, many of the institutions that have worked out the particulars of dual-career hiring report that they would extend the same opportunities to spouses and unmarried partners. There are a handful that will hire spouses but not unmarried partners, and when we discuss these institutions we intentionally refer only to "spouses." The political implications of accommodating both spouses and unmarried partners will be explored in later chapters. To assist readers, we will define other important terms as we use them within the book.

2 | Dual-Career Couples

Who Does What and Why

Our initial insights into dual-career couples in higher education were derived largely from the experiences of colleagues who were themselves academic couples, along with a few journal articles and book chapters. As our interest in academic couples deepened, we realized there were no large-scale policy studies on the topic. Most of the research in higher education approached the issue from the perspective of the couple rather than that of the academic institution. Our response was to develop a survey seeking information about policies for hiring spouses and partners for faculty positions, and more generally about the range of services available to assist dual-career couples within higher education. We sent the survey to chief academic officers at institutions belonging to the Association of American Colleges and Universities (AAC&U). Over six hundred public and private colleges and universities belong to AAC&U, representing research universities, doctoral degree granting universities, comprehensive colleges and universities, and liberal arts colleges. The response rate for this study was 360 out of 617 schools, or 59 percent, providing a fairly representative sample compared with the AAC&U population. In this chapter we report what the survey revealed. A more detailed description of the survey method is found in appendix A.

At the time we developed our survey, it was not known how many colleges and universities had developed policies related to dual-career couples. Our survey was intended in part to yield this most basic information. We defined "policy" broadly as "written and unwritten, customary, systematic approaches to assist the spouse or partner of a faculty hire." We chose this definition because we thought institutions might have long-standing practices that constitute de facto policies, even if unwritten. In this chapter we make a

An earlier version of this chapter appeared in the *Journal of Higher Education*, 71, 3 (2000): 291–321.

distinction between formal policy and ad hoc practice, although we left it to our respondents to decide whether their practice was sufficiently regularized for them to consider it a policy. As such, some of the institutions with ad hoc policies may be as regularized as those that chose to define their unwritten practice as a policy. Nonetheless, we make comparisons between those with and without policies, recognizing that this distinction is somewhat blurry.

Institutions' Willingness to Help

Most institutions consider the needs of dual-career couples important and are willing to offer them some type of assistance. The vast majority of colleges in our sample—approximately 80 percent—regard spouse and partner accommodations as at least "somewhat important" on a scale of 1 (unimportant) to 5 (very important). Of the 360 responses to our survey, 24 percent (75) reported having dual-career accommodation policies. Of colleges and universities with such policies, 42 percent (30) had them in writing, while 58 percent (42) reported having unwritten policies or practices. Fewer than 10 institutions reported implementing their policies before 1984; most did so after 1985. Among institutions that said they had no policy, only 15 percent (25) said they would "do nothing" to assist a faculty member who requested a spouse or partner accommodation. In other words, most institutions will do something to help faculty members find employment for their spouses or partners regardless of whether they have a policy. Most institutions, however, assist spouses or partners ad hoc rather than by means of a formal policy or regularized practice. Although one can argue that helping couples in this way constitutes a de facto policy, because respondents reported these practices to be irregular we have chosen to count these institutions as not having a policy.

Research Universities

As table 1 illustrates, research universities were significantly more likely than other types of institutions to report that accommodating spouses or partners is important. They were also more likely to have a dual-career policy (see table 2). This finding is in line with the conclusion drawn by Raabe (1997). Of the research universities in our sample, 45 percent had a policy, either written or unwritten. Slightly more than 20 percent of the liberal arts colleges that responded to the survey also had policies. Fewer than 20 percent of the doctoral degree granting and comprehensive colleges and universities reported having policies. While we do not know for certain why dual-career accommodations are more prevalent at research universities, we speculate that it is because of their relatively larger size, the likelihood that they have more resources at their disposal (even in times of fiscal constraint), and most important, that they recruit faculty from a national pool of applicants. Research universities exist in a competitive environment that makes them want to recruit and retain the "best" faculty. Much has been written about how research universities, especially those striving to improve their academic reputations relative to other research universities, want to recruit faculty members with the most prestigious academic pedigrees (Birnbaum 1983; Burke 1988). Given the competitive environment in which research universities operate, it is not surprising that they are more likely than other institutional types to have dual-career accommodation policies.

TABLE 1 Importance of responding to the needs of dual-career couples by institution type (scale 1–5, 5 = very important)

Institution type	Instititutions with policies (mean)
Research universities	4.67
Doctoral degree granting institutions	3.40
Comprehensive institutions	3.67
Liberal arts colleges	3.94

$F = 6.01; p<.01.$

TABLE 2 Percentage and distribution of institutions that have dual-career policies by institution type

Institution type	Policy	No policy
Research universities	45% (23)	55% (28)
Doctoral degree granting institutions	15% (5)	85% (28)
Comprehensive institutions	17% (19)	93% (90)
Liberal arts colleges	23% (31)	77% (102)

$\chi^2 = 16.74; p<.001.$

Despite differences by institutional type in how important assisting dual-career couples is considered to be, comments made by respondents at institutions of all types reflect the widespread belief that the number of dual-career couples has increased dramatically and that employment decisions are frequently made with concern for both partners' career aspirations. In part, colleges and universities see spouse and partner accommodation as important in light of these facets of contemporary work life. But seeing this as important also entails the perception that accommodating faculty spouses and partners advances an institution's hiring goals and, conversely, that inattention to such accommodation thwarts them.

Attracting the Initial Hire

Colleges and universities are most likely to offer dual-career assistance when they really want to recruit the initial hire. Even before our survey, we knew that some institutions accommodated some spouses and partners of initial faculty hires. What we did not know was whether certain categories of initial hires were more or less likely to receive consideration for their spouses or partners. Hence respondents were asked to indicate how likely they were on a scale of 1 (least likely) to 5 (most likely) to assist several groups of faculty in finding positions for their spouses or partners. Institutions with dual-career policies said they were most likely to assist the spouses or partners of initial hires in the following order: faculty of color, full professors, women professors, associate professors, accompanying spouses or partners in a department other than that of the initial hire, assistant professors, administrators, and accompanying spouses or partners in the same department as the initial hire (see table 3).

Institutions without dual-career accommodation policies stated that when they offered ad hoc assistance to a couple they were most likely to help a spouse or partner if the initial hire was a faculty member of color, a full professor, or a woman, in that order. Not surprisingly, institutions without policies were less likely than those with policies to help the spouse or partner of any category of faculty recruit. The case studies discussed in subsequent chapters, however, reveal that the primary criterion institutions use in determining whether to assist dual-career couples is how much the institution wants the initial hire. In practice we found no consistent patterns in offering assistance related to other characteristics of either initial hires or their accompanying partners or spouses.

TABLE 3 Mean likelihood of assisting by descriptor of initial hires
(scale of 1–5, 5 = most likely)

Initial hire	Policy	No policy
Faculty of color	3.77	3.13
Full professors	3.70	2.82
Women professors	3.68	2.94
Associate professors	3.58	2.66
Accompanying spouse in different department	3.56	2.77
Assistant professors	3.55	2.63
Administrators	3.28	2.63
Accompanying spouse in same department	3.08	2.12

Domestic Partners

Domestic partners are "quietly" included in many dual-career policies. Respondents were asked whether their dual-career policy or practice includes helping domestic partners find employment, and 55 percent of those with policies said they would assist domestic partners as well as spouses. Institutions offered several definitions of domestic partner. Some institutions, for example, said they let initial hires create their own definition. As one respondent explained, "For this purpose, the candidate would define it [a partner] by indicating that their decision to accept a position would be affected by this person's [the partner's] finding a job locally." Other institutions use a more legalistic definition. For example, one respondent stated, "[The] employee is required to sign a statement verifying the relationship." Along similar lines, another respondent said that partners must provide "tangible evidence of a long-term relationship such as a joint mortgage or will." Another respondent pointed out, however, that when it comes to helping a domestic partner find a job, the definition is "looser" than that used in determining who gets other benefits such as health care coverage. This may be because the assistance provided is less tangible than other types of benefits. Most of the institutions that offer domestic partner accommodations do so for both same-sex and heterosexual partners who live together. As one provost explained, "Gay, straight or otherwise—if they live together we would try to help." In fact, only three institutions that claimed to assist domestic partners said their policy excluded unmarried heterosexuals, since they could marry, but included "live-in partners who are precluded by law from official marriage." As we report later in discussing our case studies, many institutions seem willing to offer dual-career unmarried partners the same help they give spouses. Nonetheless, it appears that they do not call attention to this fact or talk about it readily. Rather, the approach taken by most seems to be that they will try to accommodate an unmarried partner "on request." We speculate that the quiet nature of this aspect of dual-career accommodation is an attempt to avoid criticism from individuals representing the full array of political viewpoints regarding marriage and partnership concerns.

The Frequency of Requests for Dual-Career Accommodations

Most colleges and universities are faced with requests for dual-career accommodations. From the outset, we thought that a key part of understanding the dual-career problem would be determining how many faculty actually request help for a spouse or partner and assessing institutions' responses to such requests. Thus we asked respondents to report on the percentage of faculty who had requested accommodations and the percentage they had tried to assist. To give an accurate picture of the range of accommodations provided, we found it necessary to examine both those institutions with policies or practices and those that reported having no formal policy. Some interesting differences emerged, as can be seen in tables 4 and 5.

TABLE 4 Percentage and distribution of initial hires requesting spouse or partner accommodations

	None	1–25%	26–50%	51–75%	76–100%
Policy	13% (9)	73% (50)	13% (9)	1% (1)	0
No policy	34% (73)	61% (133)	4% (9)	1% (1)	0

TABLE 5 Percentage and distribution of accompanying spouses or partners who were offered some form of dual-career assistance

	None	1–25%	26–50%	51–75%	76–100%
Policy	6% (4)	53% (35)	5% (3)	5% (3)	31% (21)
No policy	15% (25)	49% (80)	6% (9)	7% (11)	23% (38)

Requests at Institutions with Dual-Career Policies

Institutions with dual-career policies receive more requests for accommodation than do those without such policies. Of those institutions with dual-career accommodation policies, only 13 percent reported no requests during the past five years, compared with one-third of those with no policies. In fact, looking at the mean response to this question, one notices that institutions with policies are more likely to have received requests for accommodations than those without them. However, only 14 percent of institutions with dual-career policies reported that more than 25 percent of faculty hires asked for help in finding work for their spouses or partners. From these data we conclude that colleges and universities with accommodation policies received a large number of such requests, although they were not swamped. As one would expect, institutions without policies received far fewer requests for accommodations.

Institutions' Attempts to Fulfill Requests for Help

When dual-career accommodations are requested, institutions will try to help. Institutions both with and without policies tried to help many faculty who asked for accommodations. Over half (53 percent) of those with policies reported attempting to find jobs for between 1 and 25 percent of those who requested assistance. Of those institutions without such policies, 49 percent also reported helping between 1 and 25 percent of those who asked. On the other hand, 31 percent of those with policies, and 23 percent of those without them, reported trying to fulfill between 76 and 100 percent of the requests they received. In other words, most institutions in our study, those with and those without dual-career hiring policies, were willing to help at least some accompanying spouses or partners find work. As expected, institutions that have dual-career policies are more likely to help a higher percentage of couples than those without such policies.

Motivations for Accommodation

The goals of recruiting and retaining the best faculty members represent the key motivation for implementing dual-career accommodation policies. The main reason institutions of higher education are willing to help dual-career couples is that they see doing so as important to recruitment and retention. Very few respondents said they support accommodation policies for reasons other than to recruit and retain desired faculty. The few who did give other reasons most often mentioned "supporting family values." The following response from an institution with a spouse and partner accommodation policy was typical: "[If] we want to attract top candidates, we have to accommodate their spouses, who themselves often are in academia. In other words, we have to be competitive relative to what other universities are doing."

Competition for job applicants is also a concern to colleges and universities that do not have formal dual-career policies. As one college's chief academic officer said, "[Our lack of spouse or partner accommodations] can negatively impact our ability to recruit and retain employees. It has already had an impact." Another noted, "It is becoming increasingly difficult to hire faculty at the senior level without running into spouse or partner situations."

There is also a perception that accommodating spouses and partners may enhance recruitment and retention indirectly by boosting faculty morale and compensating for lower salaries or fewer benefits. As one respondent remarked: "Our non-competitive salaries make 'benefits' in any form significant to both recruitment and retention." Supporting families was mentioned by some chief academic officers, as typified in this comment: "Our university is committed to 'family values'—[we desire to] ease the stress and pressures on academic couples who both seek employment, especially if they must relocate."

Based on the comments on our survey, we conclude that the vast majority of chief academic officers recognized that accommodating spouses and partners of highly desirable faculty would help the institution recruit and retain faculty and might also have other positive effects. A further examination of the goals of implementing a dual-career accommodation policy illustrates that being competitive is important for those at all institutional types, that research universities have policies to attract "stars," and that institutions in more isolated locations have created policies to compensate for the lack of employment opportunities in the area.

Being Competitive in Faculty Recruitment

Being competitive in faculty recruitment is the key goal of most dual-career policies. As table 6 demonstrates, for institutions with such policies there was a significant difference in the relative importance of several goals. Respondents were asked to rate the five common goals listed below on a scale of 1 (unimportant) to 4 (very important). Statistical analysis reveals that the general goal "to be competitive" was significantly more important than

TABLE 6 Reasons for having a dual-career policy
(scale 1–4, 4 = very important)

Reason	Instititutions with policies (mean)
To be competitive	3.26
To attract faculty of color	3.05
To attract women faculty	2.91
To attract "stars"	2.68
To compensate for location	2.30

$F = 5.14; p<.01.$

other goals. Attracting faculty of color was the next most important goal, followed by "attracting women faculty," and attracting faculty "stars."

Attracting "Stars"

Research universities are more likely to care about attracting "stars" than other institutional types. There were also some statistically significant differences between institutional types with regard to other policy goals (see table 7). Specifically, research universities were significantly more likely than comprehensive institutions to say that attracting women faculty was a goal. Further, research universities were more likely than both comprehensive institutions and liberal arts colleges to point out the importance of attracting faculty stars. There were no institutional differences in the goals of attracting faculty of color and being competitive. These goals were relatively important among all sectors of higher education. At first glance, that all institutional types having dual-career hiring policies have them in order to be competitive may seem contrary to our earlier assertions about research universities. On closer inspection, however, we come to understand that what it means to be "competitive" varies across institution types. Of course administrators at regional institutions want to attract the best faculty they can, but they also want to attract those who are interested in and committed to their institutional mission. Regional institutions do not seek research stars, but they do want to hire the best faculty they can get—often defined in terms of teaching ability rather than research expertise. Dual-career hiring policies allow institutions of different types to attract and retain the best faculty as appropriate for their institutional contexts.

Institutional Location

Location is a factor in determining the need for a dual-career policy. Location, or more specifically the presence or absence of employment opportunities outside the hiring institution, bears considerably on whether spouse or partner accommodation is thought to be important. Institutions in areas with ample employment opportunities tend to see little need for a spouse or partner accommodation policy. Presumably, they can meet their recruitment and retention goals without offering such assistance. Of the colleges and universities in our study with dual-career policies, 46 percent said that "compensating for location" was an important goal; there were no significant differences by institution type. As one respondent stated, "[The] issue of spousal accommodation is unimportant only because we are experiencing no demand. We are located in a large metropolitan area with high job growth. Hence, spouses or partners have no difficulties finding employment opportunities." This sentiment was echoed by a respondent at another institution, "[Our] large metropolitan area affords ample opportunity for spousal accommodation. This is not the issue that it would be in areas where the college or university is the only game in town."

Conversely, colleges and universities in areas where there are few other employment options regard spouse or partner accommodation as considerably more important. Such institutions perceive it as a means of compensating for a lack of job opportunities in other academic institutions or out-

TABLE 7 Reasons for having a dual-career policy by institutional type
(scale 1–4, 4 = very important)

	Research universities	Doctoral degree granting institutions	Comprehensive instititutions	Liberal arts colleges	F value
To be competitive	3.60	3.00	3.14	3.15	2.45
To attract faculty of color	3.45	3.00	2.92	2.88	1.78
To attract "stars"	3.47	2.80	2.14	2.42	7.79**
To attract women faculty	3.45	2.60	2.57	2.80	3.93**
To compensate for location	2.33	3.00	2.07	2.32	805

**$p < .05$.

side higher education. In the words of one chief academic officer, "We are not located in a large urban area, and without accommodation on our part the likelihood of success in hiring is greatly decreased." As these comments clearly suggest, location bears on the perceived need to accommodate spouses or partners in relation to institutions' personnel goals—in particular, their goal of attracting and retaining desirable faculty.

How Institutions Help Dual-Career Couples

Colleges and universities offer assistance to dual-career couples in a variety of ways. Both those that state they have a policy and those that claim they lack even a regular practice employ a variety of approaches to helping accompanying spouses or partners find employment. As we noted earlier, over one-quarter (40) of those who stated they had no dual-career policy said they do help faculty spouses or partners find jobs when asked. We make the assumption that such institutions assisted spouses and partners but did not consider this practice regular enough to be a policy. Some of the provosts at institutions without accommodation policies said they helped everyone who asked, while others explained that they helped ad hoc.

Responses to the quantitative portion of the survey (table 8) show that the most common method of assisting a dual-career couple, whether or not there is a formal accommodation policy, is to provide contacts outside the institution. Making contacts inside the institution is the next most common approach, followed by sending out a résumé or vita, finding the accompanying spouse or partner a non-tenure-track position, allowing couples to share a single faculty position, and finding or creating a tenure-track faculty position. This pattern holds true for institutions both with and without dual-career policies, although the former are more likely to offer each of these forms of assistance. If institutions are going to offer assistance to an accompanying spouse or partner, they are most likely to do so once an offer has been made to the initial job candidate (table 9). Respondents could well do more than one of the things listed in table 8, and they might offer assistance at more than one point in the recruiting process, depending on the situation.

Qualitative Responses by Chief Academic Officers

Comments by chief academic officers offer more detail on how couples are accommodated. Their qualitative responses mirror those found in the quantitative sections described above. Specifically, institutions reported five general methods of helping spouses or partners find employment: helping the spouse or partner find work outside the university; hiring the accompanying spouse in an adjunct, part-time, or non-tenure-track position; allowing a couple to share a faculty position; finding or creating an administrative position within the institution; and finding the accompanying spouse a tenure-track position.

Work Outside the University

Some institutions help spouses or partners of initial hires find work outside the university. This aid takes a number of forms, from passive assistance (providing information), to somewhat more active involvement (sending résumés). Some institutions have relocation offices that provide comprehensive services. Those with a dual-career policy typically use the more active

TABLE 8 Percent and distribution of type of assistance offered

Type of assistance	Policy	No policy
Provide outside contacts	86% (68)	64% (167)
Provide inside contacts	79% (62)	61% (160)
Send vita	76% (60)	44% (116)
Create a shared position	43% (34)	20% (51)
Create a non-tenure-track position	38% (30)	16% (42)
Create a tenure-track position	20% (16)	6% (16)
None	6% (5)	10% (25)

TABLE 9 Stage in the hiring process when spouse or partner assistance typically occurs

Stage	Policy	No policy
During advertising phase	6% (4)	7% (12)
During interview phase	47% (34)	33% (61)
When offer is made	74% (54)	66% (121)
When offer is accepted	59% (43)	45% (83)
Any time	53% (39)	36% (66)

forms—although both those with policies and those without are typically willing to provide some level of assistance to accompanying spouses or partners seeking employment outside the university. The most common method of helping spouses or partners find positions outside the institution was to send letters or make phone calls on their behalf. Approximately twenty-five respondents stated that they help by using institutional networks and connections.

Several respondents said they have set up formal consortia to assist dual-career couples. As one respondent stated, "We are a member of a network of local employers who communicate regularly. . . . We route résumés, set up informational interviews, and brainstorm possibilities for candidates." Another institution set up a dual-career program called the Area Spousal Employment Assistance Program that involved nearly one hundred nearby businesses and universities as a means of sharing job information for dual-career couples. Other forms of assistance include providing access to the university employment office for job counseling, résumé advice, or job listings; sending the accompanying spouse or partner information such as position announcements and classified advertisements; and paying for the accompanying spouse to visit the campus to look for work.

Formal relocation programs or offices like these are becoming more common. Consequently, we devote chapter 4 to describing these programs in more depth.

Adjunct, Part-Time, and Non-Tenure-Track Positions

Another common means of helping dual-career couples is to find the accompanying spouse or partner a faculty position that is not permanent or that is non-tenure-track or part-time. Thirty-nine respondents described hiring a spouse or partner in a temporary position as a "typical" dual-career accommodation. At a research university, for example, "One female professor was hired in the college of Law. The trailing spouse wanted part-time employment until his Ph.D. was completed. I contacted the director of a program located in the Arts and Sciences College. Both the Dean and the Director were interested in him, based on a review of his vita. . . . He was offered a half-time non-tenure-track position."

This strategy was not unique to research universities. The dean at a comprehensive institution replied, "We hired the primary spouse to a full-time position and used the trailing spouse . . . as a part-time faculty member, constructing the load from other part-time faculty who only taught a single course." Several institutions mentioned hiring accompanying spouses or partners as sabbatical replacements for tenure-track faculty members. Occasionally these part-time positions are funded as part of a dual-career policy. For example, at one research university, the provost noted that her office provides $10,000, which the dean's office matches with funds from the dual-career program faculty fellowship. These funds are used to hire qualified spouses or partners for adjunct faculty positions. These types of strategies for accommodating spouses or partners are discussed in more detail in chapter 5.

Shared Faculty Positions

Allowing a couple to share a faculty position is another policy option. When asked to describe a "typical" accommodation, twenty institutions said they had created a shared position for a faculty member and his or her spouse or partner. Although this response to dual-career faculty couples occurs in all types of colleges and universities, it seems to be more prevalent at smaller colleges. At one liberal arts college, for instance, a tenure-track faculty member in her fourth year asked to share her position with her husband, who had a doctorate in the same field; she is now employed two-thirds time, and he works one-third time. A respondent from another liberal arts college claimed that "the basic form of arrangement [his institution uses in making dual-career accommodations] involves converting a full position to two three-quarter positions" that a couple can share. In the case of a shared appointment, institutions were clear that details must be laid out in advance, such as benefits, evaluation procedures, and what would happen if one member of the couple was not granted tenure or if the couple separated.

Institutions that created shared positions also said they had to make sure that the credentials of the spouses or partners of the initial hires met the departments' standards. A research university elaborated on allowing a couple to share a position by explaining that when a couple requested a "line split," as it is sometimes called, the department is polled. Approval of a shared position by the department chair required the "unanimous approval" of the department faculty. At another institution, a respondent said they would create a shared position only under certain conditions: "[If] we want to keep that faculty member; [if] the department is willing to give up one-third of a position; [if] the relevant department wants a spouse in a two-thirds position; [if] the relevant department and administration conduct interviews and find the spouse compares favorably with recent tenure-track people; and [if] there is sufficient enrollment in [the] spouse's area to sustain an extra two-thirds staffing."

In some instances shared positions appear to meet the needs of both dual-career couples and the institution. One respondent explained, "Job sharing has led to several successful tenured teams. . . . We have four FTE [full-time equivalents] but eight people, talents, personalities, research and teaching areas." Benefits to the college or university accruing from shared positions, however, can be disadvantageous for the couple, as one respondent noted: "Faculty two-thirds positions almost always make more than two-thirds contribution to the university." He added, however, "[The] trailing spouse has always been fully accepted, though hired unusually, the initial hire stays, and both partners are productive." Shared positions are discussed more fully in chapter 6.

Administrative Positions

Finding or creating an administrative position represents a popular solution to the dual-career dilemma. Creating or finding a "suitable" administrative job on campus was an option described as "typical" by a handful of institutions in our survey. That 78 percent of those who have policies say they are at least somewhat likely to help find work for an accompanying spouse or partner who is looking for an administrative position exemplifies the popularity of this option. Of those who do not have a dual-career policy or regular practice, 55 percent said they also assist spouses or partners looking for administrative employment. A respondent at a research university described the following typical scenario: "A recent biology hire has a wife with an MA in counseling. [We] immediately contacted the Office of Student Affairs to assess their needs. When responses were positive, we used the information to our advantage in convincing the faculty member to accept the position." At a liberal arts college, the wife of an assistant professor needed employment: "She has a master's degree and became the secretary to the dean of the College of Arts and Sciences." Sometimes the accompanying spouse or partner does not find an administrative position attractive. At a research university the provost offered this scenario: "A new assistant professor prospect had received an offer and we found a reasonable job in administration for her husband. She did not accept our offer." The provost explained that while the institution viewed the administrative position as a "reasonable job," the spouse of the assistant professor wanted a tenure-track position. This example shows that not every attempt at accommodation is successful from the viewpoint of the couple being accommodated. We do not dedicate an entire chapter to this solution (finding administrative positions), but we do cover it further in chapter 4 when we discuss relocation services.

Tenure-Track Positions

Finding the accompanying spouse or partner a tenure-track position is rare, but it does occur, especially at research universities. In a few instances, institutions attempt to either find or create tenure-track positions for accompanying spouses or partners. In rare cases, both faculty members have "gotten lucky" and received tenure-track positions at the same institution with no intervention. At one research university, the provost described a scenario where the spouse of a faculty member hired in the humanities was subsequently hired in the college of physical and mathematical sciences. No one had interceded on her behalf. In some cases the tenure-track job becomes available to an accompanying spouse after a few years as an adjunct or a lecturer. For example, the provost at a comprehensive institution described hiring a faculty member on the tenure track and offering the spouse a lecturer or non-tenure-track position. He added, "Now a position has opened, and the spouse has moved to a tenure-track position." Another provost explained, "A couple of years ago a potential faculty member in Business had a 'trailing spouse' who was given a non-tenure-track position. The next year she chose to go through a search process for a tenure-track position rather than exercise the spousal option even though the college was willing to appoint her. She felt she would be stigmatized without the search." She received the position.

Several institutions, all large research universities, have developed complex funding formulas to create new faculty positions for select spouses or partners. In one case an English department offered an assistant professorship to a person whose spouse had just completed a degree in history. The dean of the College of Liberal Arts gave a new line to the history department and offered to pay one-third of the expense from college funds if the history department and the English department together paid the rest from their budgets. The hire was made. Two other institutions in our sample also said that the cost of a new faculty line could be divided equally between three units—the provost, the department making the initial hire, and the partner's department. As one explained, "When we make an accommodation that involves funding a position, we try to use a cost-sharing approach. Ideally [the cost of the new line is divided in the following manner:] one-third hiring unit, one-third faculty member's unit, one-third provost. Fairly frequently the allocation will change . . . with a decreasing amount paid by the provost. As a general rule, we limit dual-career funding to three years." Cost sharing in this manner is purposeful and allows the department hiring the accompanying spouse or partner the time to find the resources to gradually support the position with its own resources.

For obvious reasons, providing tenure-track positions for accompanying spouses or partners, while probably the ideal for the faculty couple, is the most controversial and least available of the dual-career assistance methods used by colleges and universities. Several universities do have policies that allow for creating tenure-track positions for spouses or partners, mostly on a limited basis. Because a tenure-track position is often a faculty spouse or partner's ultimate goal, a good deal of the discussion surrounding the pros and cons of dual-career policies concerns this one strategy, and it is this strategy that receives the lion's share of attention from supporters and critics alike. We discuss this form of accommodation in more detail in chapter 8.

Barriers to Dual-Career Policies

Colleges and universities with dual-career policies face barriers when instituting and implementing them. Because we sensed that many institutions would like to develop policies but have few models to follow, we were also interested in these barriers. Of the seventy-nine institutions reporting that they had a policy, fifty-four responded to an open-ended question regarding barriers. Of these, nine reported facing no barriers, in large part because they described their policies as fairly weak and ineffective. For example, one said, "The policy does not achieve a great deal or guarantee anything, so it was easy to create." Another respondent explained that his institution had not faced a barrier because there had been no call for using the policy. He explained: "There might be difficulties in instituting a more formal policy. The provost has suggested that we might respond to particular situations by helping to create some positions for spouses, but since that suggestion was made, no appropriate situation has arisen. So far, no accommodations." Respondents from two research universities asserted with apparent pride that they faced no problems. One said, "None. Administration supplied $500,000 start-up money." Another said, "None, really, and we received enthusiastic support from the Office of Equal Opportunity when our policy was created." Another did not see that the policy had caused any major shift in activity. "None, really, but it is very limited, and we were already doing most of these things informally."

Most of the respondents from institutions that have a spouse or partner accommodation policy said they faced barriers when creating the policy and again later when trying to implement it. We categorized the real and perceived barriers identified by those institutions having policies as follows: communication, coordination, and administrative concerns; concerns over departmental autonomy; concerns for equity; concerns about the quality of an accompanying spouse or partner; and other. It is important to note at the outset that most of these barriers assume that the policy in question involves hiring a spouse or partner into an academic unit while forgoing a regular search process. Respondents did not cite barriers to other types of dual-career accommodations, such as relocation services.

Communication, Coordination, and Administrative Barriers

The following are representative of the types of communication, coordination, and administrative barriers institutions encountered in implementing a dual-career accommodation policy that involves hiring an accompanying spouse or partner at the college or university. These perceived barriers impeded policy formation and also implementation. Respondents at several institutions talked about the labor-intensive nature of having such an accommodation policy. For example, one provost explained that the difficulties they faced stemmed from "coordination with our Human Resources office, time, and effort on their part and those in the academic administration to set up the program." Another outlined the range of difficulties faced to make a policy work: "(1) Developing a system for learning about job openings on campus and in the community; (2) enlisting the cooperation of the dean, directors and department heads; and (3) working with search committees to make them aware of our services." Several provosts also pointed to potential coordination and communication problems such as "difficulties working between and among departments and between and among colleges" when attempting to make accommodations. Again, most of these concerns imply that the college or university is hiring the accompanying spouse or partner. The time it takes to create and implement a dual-career policy—especially one that involves creating tenure-track positions—is a true barrier, but one that is often viewed as being worth the trouble. As we discuss in subsequent chapters, such processes not only are workable but, if enacted judiciously, can improve communication across academic units. Most important, creating an appropriate dual-career hiring policy is likely to help institutions recruit and retain the faculty they want.

Departmental Autonomy

Dual-career hiring policies can be perceived as negatively affecting departmental autonomy. Not unexpectedly, faculty resistance and department autonomy were thought to be major barriers to creating and implementing dual-career policies, especially when the policy involves hiring an accompanying spouse or partner. The words of one provost sum up the nature of this barrier: "Departmental autonomy and right of refusal stops us from hiring more couples and probably slowed [the creation of] a policy." Even more prevalent were responses indicating various forms of resistance, individual or departmental, to such dual-career hiring policies. The following response demonstrates this problem: "Some current faculty members feel such accommodation places colleges in a 'hostage' situation and/or shows unfair favor to one member of a department or college." Another added, "The faculty are *not* in favor of creating positions for spouses. Other factors are more important to them in resource allocation." The case studies presented throughout this book highlight the means different institutions have used to minimize threats to departmental autonomy. The most noteworthy strategy to minimize such threats is to not force an academic unit to hire someone they do not perceive as qualified for the position. The policies highlighted in this book allow departments complete autonomy in deciding whether to hire an accompanying spouse or partner. Failure to pay attention to the need for faculty autonomy in hiring decisions is likely to lead to significant problems for the individuals hired under such a policy, for the administration, and for the policy itself.

Concerns about Equity

Some chief academic officers expressed concerns about equity in implementing their policies. A few institutions mentioned fears that an accommodation policy focusing on the institution's hiring an accompanying spouse or partner would be at odds with a commitment to equity in hiring. These institutions reported concerns such as "charges or perceptions of favoritism," "concerns about nepotism, favoritism, and conflict of interest," and "equity —usually making accommodations for spouses seen as a detriment to hiring faculty of color and women." Generally speaking, institutions with dual-career hiring policies have created some safeguards in their policies that protect them from violating basic notions of equity. For example, in most institutions with dual-career hiring policies, direct hires are screened by the institutional equal opportunity officer to make sure the hire does not negatively affect the institution's affirmative action goals. Equity concerns are exacerbated when policies are not in writing and are applied too selectively. These mechanisms are discussed throughout the remaining chapters, with special attention devoted to this concern in chapter 9.

Quality of the Accompanying Spouse or Partner

The qualifications of the accompanying spouse or partner were also seen as a problem at several institutions—especially when the accommodation in question involves hiring that person. One administrator stated the concern quite bluntly. He explained that the barrier his institution faced was rooted in the "fear that so-called part-timers would not be 'real' professionals." Another provost reported that the basic concern was about the "ability of the spouse compared to the ability of [the initial] faculty member." He implied that the accompanying spouse or partner would be less qualified than the recruit being sought. One respondent was more concerned that the overall quality of the institution could be hurt if dual-career accommodations in the form of direct hires occurred too frequently. He cited "department integrity and quality concerns" as the barrier to policy formation. As we discuss in subsequent chapters, especially chapter 9, concerns about quality are real but have been overcome by institutions that have implemented dual-career hiring policies. The main antidote to resolving concerns about quality is to make sure that spouses and partners of initial hires are not foisted on departments without their consent. It is exceedingly important that faculty have a say in whether an accompanying spouse or partner has sufficient qualifications— especially if accommodation involves any type of faculty position.

Reasons for Not Having Formal Policies

Institutions without policies offered a variety of reasons why they were not formally assisting dual-career couples. We knew before writing our survey instrument that there were institutions that did not assist dual-career couples. The survey, we hoped, would help us understand the reasons behind decisions not to offer such assistance. If institutions said they did not help spouses or partners of initial hires find positions, we asked them why. As expected, those without policies had many reasons, which fell into several major categories: there is no demand for accommodation; the institution lacks the resources to offer assistance; such accommodations raise equity concerns; legal concerns and institutional policies that preclude dual-career accommodation; and inertia and faculty resistance are barriers to policy creation. Again, most if not all of the responses to this question focused on helping a spouse or partner find work at the institution rather than work in the community.

Lack of Demand

The most frequently given reason for not having a policy was that there is no need or demand. For example, an administrator at one master's degree granting university replied, "The need has not arisen. We would try to assist if feasible." Respondents at several urban institutions said they had no need for a policy because there were so many employment opportunities in their area. For example, an administrator at a master's degree granting institution said they had no need [because] "we are located in a high-density area with lots of job opportunities." Some simply replied, "No need." Based on commonly used statistics indicating that 80 percent of all professionals have spouses or partners who also work, it is likely that these institutions have not been asked to accommodate spouses or partners, not that there is no need. Location of the college or university is also a likely explanation.

Lack of Resources

Some provosts reported that their institutions lacked the resources to offer assistance. Small size, lack of positions and resources, or both were other reasons given for not helping spouses or partners of faculty recruits find work. One respondent simply said, "[We don't have] enough positions to accommodate [a spouse or partner]." Another explained further, "Our [bachelor's degree granting] university is small and lacks the power to create budget supported positions for employment." While institutional size and resources can limit the approach used to assist dual-career couples, there are some dual-career policies that can be enacted in these cases. Specifically, institutions with limited resources may want to consider sharing advertising with other institutions in the region (see chapter 7), or they might consider allowing couples to share a single position (see chapter 6).

Concerns about Fairness

A handful of those without policies raised concerns about the fairness of dual-career accommodation. A respondent from one research university stated, "All positions are open to competition." Another said, "We recruit the best faculty we can find for all open positions." Similarly, another explained, "The long-standing practice of [the university] is to hire spouses entirely on their own individual merits and not to hire husband and wife teams. We also do not allow a spouse to be in a reporting relationship to his or her spouse." So, while some universities view spouse and partner accommodation as a means to promote equity by helping them recruit women and faculty of color, others view equity and fairness as precisely the reasons not to have a dual-career accommodation policy. Concerns about fairness and equity are discussed in more detail in chapter 9.

Concerns about Legality

Some provosts raised concerns about the legality of dual-career hiring policies. Institutions that had no dual-career accommodation policy often cited the law as an explanation. Note that according to Shoben (1997), who examined dual-career policies from a legal perspective, there have been no recorded legal challenges to existing dual-career hiring policies at colleges and universities. Nonetheless, a respondent at a research university listed his reason for not having a policy as "affirmative action and the expectation of open competition." Such a comment implies a worry that accommodating an accompanying spouse or partner might involve granting a position without conducting a formal search, which could then affect affirmative action goals. Similarly, other respondents believed there were legal barriers to formal dual-career hiring policies—especially if they involved forgoing an open search. As one respondent explained, "Our general counsel believes there are legal problems with Affirmative Action and Equal Opportunity laws if we had an across the board policy." Similarly, a respondent at a large urban university said his understanding of employment law was that "'opportunity hiring' programs [as might be the case in a dual-career hiring policy] may be 'the law of the land,'" but that his institution "currently prefers not to have such programs because of other legal concerns." At another institution a respondent claimed that his institution had no choice in not implementing a dual-career hiring policy. He explained, "We operate under a court settlement which requires a national search for all tenure-track positions." These responses all presuppose that the form of accommodation being discussed is hiring an accompanying spouse or partner into a faculty position rather than some other type (relocation services, shared positions, etc.).

While not a widespread concern, union contracts and state policies (or lack thereof) were also given as reasons for not assisting spouses or partners. For example, an administrator at a public master's degree granting institution explained: "Contract negotiations for system campuses preclude special [hiring] arrangements." At another institution, which is part of a large state system, the respondent stated that "[accommodation had not been] introduced into the systemwide collective bargaining agreement." Yet another explained that "policies of the Board of Trustees . . . make no provision for this." Chapter 9 discusses some of these legal concerns in more depth.

Inertia and Faculty Resistance

A few respondents suggested that institutional inertia and faculty resistance were the reasons their schools did not have a dual-career accommodation policy. One administrator admitted that at her institution "[we] haven't figured out how. . . [owing to a] lack of leadership on personnel matters." Another respondent argued that "[it's] not our problem." In some ways, these answers probably best represent the reason institutions do not yet have dual-career hiring policies. Such policies are not easy to implement, and given likely resistance by a variety of constituents, many institutional leaders choose to let inertia rather than activity be their guide. These factors may explain why so many institutions in our sample have opted for ad hoc approaches rather than creating more formal policies.

Lack of Formal Assessment of Policies

Most dual-career policies have not been formally assessed, though colleges and universities believe they are effective. Policies and practices to accommodate dual-career faculty couples are fairly new, so it is not surprising that few of the institutions in our sample had conducted a formal assessment of their effects. Nonetheless, we asked the chief academic officers to estimate the percentage of accompanying spouses or partners who found employment as a result of assistance and to estimate the percentage of initial hires who came to university because the institution helped their spouses or partners. We also asked for other views about the relative effectiveness of their policies.

Success in Finding Satisfactory Employment for Partners

Not all accompanying spouses or partners who are assisted find satisfactory employment. Institutional efforts have not always been successful. Our survey asked specifically about accommodating spouses and partners seeking employment in faculty positions, but we have no way of knowing whether respondents' answers to this question referred only to that group or also to success at finding positions off campus or finding on-campus nonfaculty positions. Of those institutions with dual-career policies, 73 percent reported finding jobs for fewer than half of those they tried to help. Of those without policies, 88 percent were able to find jobs for fewer than half of those they assisted. Conversely, 27 percent of those with policies and 12 percent of those without policies were able to find work for at least half. While institutions with accommodation policies appear to be more successful in finding employment for an accompanying spouse or partner than those without them, even they have met with only moderate success, at best.

Success in Recruiting Initial Hires

The chief academic officers responding to the survey believed that initial hires were more likely to come to the college or university if the institution tried to help their spouses or partners find employment. Half of the institutions with policies said they had been successful in hiring more than 50 percent of the recruits who requested assistance for their spouses or partners, and 36 percent of those without dual-career policies also said that helping a spouse or partner enabled them to attract at least 50 percent of the faculty they wanted to hire. We did not survey the faculty seeking positions for their spouses or partners, but it makes sense that institutional assistance does enhance efforts to recruit faculty. Our data from the case studies support this conclusion. The figures in table 11 should be understood as estimates by the chief academic officers or their designees of the effectiveness of their assistance efforts.

TABLE 10 Percentage and distribution of accompanying spouses or partners who found employment with the assistance of the hiring institution

	None	1–25%	26–50%	51–75%	76–100%
Policy	13% (8)	49% (31)	11% (7)	19% (12)	8% (5)
No policy	21% (32)	57% (83)	10% (14)	9% (13)	3% (5)

TABLE 11 Percentage and distribution of initial hires who came to the university because the institution assisted their spouse or partners

	None	1–25%	26–50%	51–75%	76–100%
Policy	8% (5)	32% (20)	10% (6)	19% (12)	31% (19)
No policy	11% (15)	45% (59)	8% (11)	15% (19)	21% (28)

Qualitative and Numerical Responses Compared

The qualitative responses to the survey mirror the numerical responses. When asked to explain in what ways their spouse and partner accommodation policy was or was not effective, most provosts said their practices were at least partly effective. Most suggested they were effective in supporting their recruiting and retention goals. One provost reported, "We have been able to hire several excellent faculty members as a result of our efforts in finding suitable employment for spouses or partners." Another described the benefits of their dual-career accommodation policy for hiring faculty of color. He credited the policy with assisting the institution in having "the highest percentage of minority faculty (14 percent) and the highest percentage of women (26 percent) we have ever had. Faculty retention is up."

Several respondents said that their practices boosted faculty morale or otherwise pleased faculty, as this comment suggests: "[Our practices] provide flexibility and serve as a positive signal that we are aware of the problems faced by dual-career couples." Similarly, another provost stated that having a dual-career policy forces the institution to pay attention to problems it previously ignored: "[Through our dual-career policy we are] recognizing issues and tailoring new and replacement positions to suit [the needs of the faculty and departments]."

Success of Ad Hoc Accommodations

Even colleges and universities without formal policies believe their ad hoc accommodations are successful in recruiting good faculty. Fifty-four institutions that do not have a spouse or partner accommodation policy, but that nevertheless try to help, also responded to the question about how their practices are effective in achieving their goals. Most such respondents claimed their ad hoc approach was at least partly effective. Most believed that their dual-career accommodation practices helped them to recruit and retain faculty, as suggested by this comment: "We have been able to make three splendid hires in the last five years that we probably would not have been able to make without this extra effort." Another respondent explained, "I think we've hired and retained female faculty as a result of these efforts." Others believed their accommodation practices boosted faculty morale. According to another provost, "[We are] effective in the sense that we show concern; good will and caring came through in our efforts to be helpful. People tend to believe that our efforts are sincere. We are ineffective in that we have failed twice in recent years to find employment for the trailing spouse." Another provost commented on her institution's effectiveness in helping the accompanying spouse or partner get a job: "Usually we can find something, though [it is often] less than ideal." Another speculated that a policy might be helpful: "If we had the money, and internal acceptance of the effort, which we don't, it would be helpful in attracting faculty to have a spousal hiring policy." In sum, helping dual-career couples find work, even ad hoc, is perceived to yield positive benefits for the institution.

Unexpected Consequences of Dual-Career Policies

Because policies and regular practices have both intended and unintended consequences, we asked respondents to identify any unexpected outcomes of their efforts to help dual-career couples. Of those institutions that responded, several said they had experienced no unintended consequences. Among institutions that had, "diminished faculty morale" was mentioned most frequently. There were a number of ways a dual-career policy lowered morale. One institution reported that morale was seriously damaged when an accompanying spouse failed to meet work expectations. The provost described the situation as consisting of "a gravely alienated faculty member whose spouse didn't work out [combined with] a seriously alienated department, unhappy because one of its members is gravely alienated."

Another provost said that their policy had inadvertently damaged morale because some faculty perceived hiring decisions as unfair: "Some . . . see spouses of higher level administrators getting appointments as unfair or inequitable." One provost mentioned a different manifestation of perceived unfairness that hurt morale: "Colleagues in small programs sometimes find a doubled vote unfair (if both spouses are in the same program)." Yet another institution thought that its policy damaged the morale of faculty who could not or did not use the policy, perhaps because they were unaware that such a policy existed or were hired before it was implemented.

Three institutions reported that divorce, while not an unintended consequence of their accommodation policy per se, created problems. One of these responded merely by noting: "Divorce has institutional consequences." One reported two instances of divorce between faculty members who had been accommodated: "We have had two cases of divorce, which is a little touchy. In one case, two individuals are still employed as faculty in different departments. In another case, the trailing spouse left a tenure-track job to go live with someone else." Divorce is seen as particularly awkward if the accommodation involves having faculty spouses or partners in the same department or school. On the other hand, failure to help couples find employment may also lead to marital problems that might affect productivity. One administrator in our survey suggested that despite an accommodation policy, a lack of employment opportunities may have contributed to a couple's breakup: "One couple divorced, in (minor) part, because little employment was available for the spouse."

Other unintended consequences include expenses of energy and time for all involved in trying to make an accommodation, lack of office and research facilities to house those who are being accommodated, tension among department chairs who are involved in hiring accompanying spouses, and resentment over failed attempts at accommodation. Often, even where a policy exists, accommodation, especially when achieved through hiring for faculty positions, depends on the cooperation of fellow administrators and faculty colleagues. If an attempt fails, the couple may be unhappy, as may be the administrators and other faculty involved.

Not all of the unintended consequences of a school's spouse or partner accommodation policy were viewed as negative. Three institutions reported that their policy had led to unanticipated benefits, as this response implies: "I can think of instances where the [accompanying] partner was considered to be a greater professional success and an asset to the university [than the initial hire]." Another added, "Despite warnings of the faculty . . . I do not know of instances of failure of the spouse to achieve tenure and to make very positive contributions to the university."

Unintended Consequences of a Lack of Dual-Career Policies

Institutions without dual-career policies also face unintended consequences. Interestingly, there were fifty-two responses to the question regarding unintended consequences from institutions that had said they had no spouse or partner accommodation policy. It is clear that some of the responses were meant to describe the unintended consequences of not having a formal policy. The most commonly mentioned unintended consequence is resentment among faculty. One reason for resentment is that, lacking a policy, spouses or partners are hired purely ad hoc and, as suggested by this response, "[the lack of a policy] may lead to unequal levels of assistance, or perceived assistance, among faculty."

The second most frequently mentioned unintended consequence is that lack of a policy undermines recruitment and retention efforts. As one respondent mentioned, "We do not have a proactive policy; therefore it is possible we miss out on extremely qualified candidates to other colleges and universities who do."

What We Learned from Our Survey

What, in a nutshell, does our survey reveal? The following summarizes what we consider to be some of the most interesting and important aspects of colleges' and universities' responses to dual-career couples.

- The needs of dual-career couples are important to colleges and universities.
- Chief academic officers believe either that demand for spouse and partner accommodations has increased over the past five years or that it has remained constant.
- Most colleges and universities are willing to offer some type of dual-career assistance when asked. Most of this assistance is offered ad hoc rather than as part of a formal written policy.
- The goal of most dual-career hiring policies is to make the institution competitive in attracting and retaining high-quality faculty members.
- Research universities are more likely than other types of colleges and universities to have dual-career policies. They are also more likely to allow for hiring an accompanying spouse or partner into a tenure-track position. This is because research universities are more likely to have the re-

sources and flexibility to offer internal positions, both academic and administrative. They are also more likely to operate in a national labor market that seeks individuals with the best academic pedigrees.

- Domestic partners (same-sex or heterosexual) are frequently included in dual-career hiring policies. However, most institutions choose not to call attention to this facet of their policies to avoid criticism from those representing various political viewpoints.
- When helping a spouse or partner find work, institutions employ five approaches. The most common solution is finding work outside the institution. Internal accommodations most frequently entail temporary rather than long-term positions as adjunct or part-time instructors.

  1. The institution may help the accompanying spouse or partner find work outside the university by active methods (use of prearranged consortia, sending résumés, making contacts) or by more passive methods (providing information to a spouse or partner). They may also create relocation offices that offer more formal and more comprehensive services.
  2. The institution may hire the accompanying spouse or partner in a part-time, adjunct, or non-tenure-track position.
  3. The institution may create a shared position in which the initial hire and the spouse or partner share a single academic line.
  4. The institution may find an internal administrative job for the accompanying spouse or partner.
  5. In rare situations, the couple may find or the college or university may create a tenure-track position for a spouse or partner.

- Colleges and universities with dual-career policies encounter barriers in creating and implementing them, especially when the policy involves hiring an accompanying spouse or partner at the institution.

  1. Communication across departments and schools involved in accommodating an accompanying spouse or partner may be a barrier.
  2. Hiring an accompanying spouse or partner may be perceived as negatively affecting departmental autonomy.
  3. Some policies may be perceived as leading to inequitable hiring practices that can thwart affirmative action goals.
  4. The quality of the accompanying spouse or partner may come into question in hiring decisions.

- Institutions lacking a dual-career policy indicated the following barriers to creating one.

    1. Some institutions experienced little or no demand for a dual-career accommodation policy.
    2. Lack of institutional resources, often as a function of size, can limit types of dual-career accommodation.
    3. Some people think dual-career policies are unfair because they favor the needs of some faculty over those of others.
    4. Some question the legality of a dual-career hiring policy.
    5. Inertia and faculty resistance may be seen as barriers to creating a dual-career hiring policy.

- Despite a lack of systematic evaluation, most schools believe their policies help them meet recruitment and retention goals. The presence of a dual-career hiring policy can improve morale among faculty when an accommodation attempt is successful. When an attempt fails or when a hire is foisted on an unwilling department, however, morale can be lowered.
- In colleges and universities without formal policies, some faculty may resent an ad hoc approach viewed as favoring some hires over others. Further, those without formal policies believe they may be at a disadvantage in recruiting some faculty candidates.
- Just because an institution tries to accommodate an accompanying spouse or partner does not mean the couple will be satisfied with the result. Successful accommodations, in which both members of the couple and the institution as a whole are completely satisfied, are rare and require some luck.

Concluding Comment

Overall, the survey results suggest that assisting dual-career couples in academia is complex. Institutions that choose to have a dual-career policy face issues such as how such a policy might affect the traditional role of the faculty in hiring their colleagues or how it affects the institution's overall hiring needs. As an example, the College of Liberal Arts and Sciences in our own university has what a newly hired faculty couple recently described as a "very family-friendly hiring policy." In 2001, however, the College had to put its own dual-career policy on hold for a year because departments made so many requests for regular faculty lines that the dean was faced with either denying what she perceived to be legitimate requests for regular lines or "saving" lines for dual-career hires. These are not simple problems. The decision in this case was to announce that all "accommodations" would have to occur within the scope of regularly defined positions. Colleges and universities need to address how to attend to the personal needs of faculty they are trying to recruit while also meeting the needs of the institution as a whole. Balancing the needs of the individual against the needs of the institution is difficult, and in many circumstances it is the individual who does not receive a completely satisfactory accommodation. Such is the nature of the problems colleges and universities face as they attempt to formulate workable dual-career policies.

These are some of the concerns we explore more fully in the chapters that follow. Data collected through in-depth site visits to several institutions that approach the needs of dual-career couples in different ways provide additional insight into the complexities of dual-career accommodation policies.

3 | Introduction to the Cases and the Qualitative Method

Chapters 4–8 are based primarily on data collected from case studies of five academic institutions that have approached the task of assisting dual-career couples in different ways. These institutions do not necessarily represent the "best" approaches, but they do serve as models of how different institutional types in different places and with differing goals go about making dual-career accommodations. In selecting the sites, we looked at the results of the survey of chief academic officers described in the previous chapter and determined the array of formal approaches. We found that approaches to assisting dual-career couples fell broadly into five categories:

1. offering relocation services primarily targeted to assisting spouses and partners in finding employment off campus
2. providing temporary, adjunct faculty positions
3. creating opportunities for shared positions
4. advertising positions jointly with nearby institutions
5. helping accompanying spouses and partners find tenure-track positions

Considering these approaches, we looked at the responses to our survey to find institutions that seemed most clearly to represent each one. In selecting sites, we also looked at location, knowing that institutions in more rural and more isolated locales would have more incentive to make dual-career accommodations. We also wanted the sites to represent a variety of institutional types, differing in size, control, mission, and resource availability. The final five sites we selected represent this diversity of institutional type. A brief description of them follows. (The institution names used here are pseudonyms.)

Wildwood College

"Wildwood" is a four-year residential, coeducational liberal arts college located in a midwestern city with a population of roughly 40,000. The nearest city of any considerable size is about forty-five miles away. The college was founded in the 1840s by a religious society; it maintains an affiliation with its religious roots, but it attracts students and faculty from all religious backgrounds. The college is small and highly selective, with just over a thousand students and slightly more than a hundred faculty members. The faculty hold terminal degrees and are expected to teach as well as to conduct research with the undergraduates. Currently, 38 percent of the full-time faculty are women, and 16 percent are people of color. The students come from all fifty states and over thirty countries, and most live on campus. The college's endowment is approximately $240 million. The campus has a number of stately brick buildings and well-maintained, wooded grounds. We selected Wildwood as a case study site because, like many other small campuses, it has opted to assist dual-career couples by creating split faculty positions in which a couple is hired for a single tenure-track position.

Heartland University

"Heartland University" describes itself as a family-friendly place. It is in an urban center of 200,000 people, surrounded by farmlands and rural communities; the nearest larger city is about an hour's drive away. Heartland is a major research university enrolling approximately 23,000 students in its eleven colleges. As a land-grant university, it is classified as a Carnegie Research I institution and is a member of the Association of American Universities. In 2000 its 1,500 faculty members brought in nearly $100 million in grants in contracts. Approximately 20 percent or 294 of its tenure-track faculty are women. Of the women faculty, 82 percent are at the assistant or associate rank. Although the number of women may be increasing, there are relatively few minority faculty at Heartland. In fall 1998 the university listed 145 faculty of color. Of these, the vast majority are Asian. Heartland represents institutions that have a formalized policy allowing for trailing academic partners to attain one-year adjunct positions in an academic department. Further, Heartland operates a spouse and partner relocation office that helps nonacademic accompanying partners find work in the local area.

Riverdale University

"Riverdale University" is also a land-grant university with a strong emphasis on agriculture and engineering. Riverdale is a big university in a relatively small city. Its main campus enrolls 37,000 students, and its six branch campuses bring the student total to about 67,000. Students can choose from over 6,500 courses in two hundred specializations offered through its twelve schools. Like Heartland, Riverdale is a Carnegie Research I University. In 1996–97, faculty and researchers at Riverdale raised and spent about $205 million on funded research. There are some four hundred research institutes within the university. Located as it is in a relatively small metropolitan area (approximately 150,000), Riverdale, with its 12,213 total employees, is the major employer, counting over 1,800 faculty and 2,000 academic administrators among its employees. Of the 1,634 tenure-track faculty, 349 are women. Although located in a small city, Riverdale is approximately one and one-half hours south of one major city and one hour north of another. It is one of two major research universities in the state. Riverdale offers two programs to assist dual-career couples—a bridge program that provides temporary funding for academic units to hire an accompanying spouse into a tenure-track position and a relocation office that helps accompanying spouses find employment in the area and assists couples in making the transition to a new community.

Belle State University

"Belle State University" is a land-grant institution, serving over 28,000 students on an expansive campus located in a thriving capital city. The faculty at Belle State number approximately 1,600 and garnered more than $88 million in federal research funding in 2001. The university is divided into nine colleges that offer more than 5,200 degrees in over a hundred fields of study. Belle State is especially well regarded for its programs in science, engineering, and technology, but it offers a conventional liberal arts curriculum as well. Its campus is attractive, with an interesting mixture of old and new architecture and an abundance of trees and flowering shrubs. Unlike some of the other campuses in this study, Belle State is located in a community with a rather large number of corporate headquarters as well as several other academic institutions within commuting distance, making it easier to find positions for accompanying partners and spouses. In fact, its location is so favorable that the city has received numerous acknowledgments for being among the most "livable" communities in the country. The institution was selected initially as a case study site because we believed it had created a consortium with other academic institutions and businesses to assist in hiring accompanying spouses or partners of academics. On our visit we learned that the consortium was not functioning. However, we learned that Belle State does make the most of its location and is willing to offer ad hoc relocation assistance. In our view, the university represented the most typical approach to dual-career accommodations in academia.

Hilltop University

"Hilltop University" is a public, research-extensive university. Founded in the late 1800s, this flagship university prides itself on being one of the best public universities in the country. The institution enrolls over 48,000 students and employs 2,700 faculty. Approximately 25 percent of the student body is enrolled in graduate or professional degree programs. More than 100 undergraduate degree programs and 1,700 graduate degree programs are offered at Hilltop, many of them ranked among the top ten in the country. Hilltop is located in a vibrant community of fewer than 100,000 residents. It was selected as a case study site because it has a regular process for hiring an accompanying spouse or partner into a tenure-track position. According to records kept by the Provost's Office at Hilltop, sixteen faculty couples had been accommodated under the dual-career policy. Respondents noted that this figure underestimates the number of academic couples on campus because it fails to account for those hires that were made without the assistance of the central administration (faculty who are both in the same department or college) and does not include academics whose spouses are employed in non-tenure-track lines. It is important to note that given the process followed under Hilltop's policy there is no record of how many accommodations were attempted but failed to culminate in job offers for both members of the couple. Whatever the actual number of dual-career faculty hires on campus, respondents made it very clear that there are many more couples at Hilltop who could benefit from some sort of hiring accommodation if it were offered.

Data Collection

To determine the nature of the different policies and assess their relative strengths and weaknesses, we visited each site and interviewed administrators who were directly involved in creating or implementing the program or policy, deans and department chairs who have worked with the policy or practice, the affirmative action officer, and academic couples who have been either successfully or unsuccessfully accommodated at the institution. A contact in the Provost's Office on each campus helped us to select and arrange our interview schedules during our two-day visits. Typical questions addressed the following issues: familiarity and experience with the policy or practice; description of the policy or practice; how it was implemented; its intended and unintended consequences; its strengths and weaknesses; and suggestions for improvement. We also conducted interviews with approximately fifteen chief academic officers at small colleges to obtain more information about dual-career hiring accommodations from their perspective. We did this latter analysis because we believed the situation at small colleges was different enough to warrant a separate investigation.

Data Analysis

In analyzing our data, we followed the constant comparative method (Strauss and Corbin 1990). Our approach was inductive, attempting to identify common themes and emerging patterns using content analysis (Patton 1980). This method of analysis is appropriate, since little is known about what motivates a particular campus to assist dual-career couples and how that motivation might translate to other campuses. In presenting our data, we are writing both within-case and between-case analyses. Each site visit provides the basis of a separate case study, recognizing the institutional context of the individual policies or practices. Such a "thick description" of the context should allow other institutions to determine if a policy at one institution can be used as a model for them to follow (Lincoln and Guba 1985). The between-case analysis is used to identify what is common among the institutions so as to generate an overall conceptual framework or theory to explain how and why dual-career policies are being enacted across institutional types.

4 | Relocation Services

Jack and Cindy have been married for ten years and have two children aged seven and five. Jack has a Ph.D. in physics and recently accepted a position as an assistant professor at Riverdale University. Although he had three offers, he and his wife liked Riverdale and the small city where it is located. It will be a good place to raise their children. Jack's wife has a master's degree in public relations and has been working at a firm in the area where the couple currently lives. Cindy definitely wants to continue working, preferably in public relations. During the interview Jack was hesitant to press too hard about the need for his wife to find a suitable job, but he was told about the relocation office during his on-campus interview and given a packet of information about the program. When he was offered the position, Jack told the chair that he very much wanted to accept but that his decision would ultimately depend on whether Cindy could find appropriate work. The department chair said he could not promise anything, but he assured Jack that he would have the relocation specialist call them immediately. Shari, the director of relocation services, called the very next day and chatted with Cindy. She had Cindy send her résumé and told her about the office's Web site, which provided detailed information about the city, businesses, and a host of other services such as schools and churches. As Jack and the chair negotiated start-up costs, salary, and such, Cindy and Shari worked on finding Cindy a job. Whenever Cindy applied for a position, Shari would write a letter of introduction to accompany her résumé and cover letter. When the time came for Jack to give an oral commitment, Cindy still hadn't had a definite offer, but Shari had put her in touch with several local firms and had sent her résumé to the public relations office on campus as well as to the sports information office. Jack and Cindy felt encouraged by the assistance Riverdale offered. Neither of the other two universities where Jack interviewed had even mentioned relocation services, although the department chair at each university was willing to send Cindy's résumé out to local companies and to give them some names to contact. So they accepted the position at Riverdale and moved to Riverdale City. Cindy continued to work with Shari, and in January she was offered a position at a local firm. In the meantime, Shari had helped them locate a neighborhood to live in, choose physicians, and even find a church.

Jack and Cindy, a fictitious composite of couples we met, were offered and took advantage of the formal relocation services provided by Riverdale University. Such services help both the initial hire and the family by offering a range of services to introduce newcomers to the community and to help them find everything from hairdressers to doctors to jobs. In the words of one relocation specialist, "The ultimate objective of spousal career assistance is to help the transferring spouse transition to a new career opportunity. The emphasis is not on the provider giving or finding the client a job; rather it is on providing spouses with the information, guidance and resources to facilitate their self-achievement of this goal." In this chapter we describe relocation services as typically found in other employment sectors such as business, the military, and the foreign service; discuss approaches typically found in higher education; and then focus on two examples from our case study sites— Heartland University and Riverdale University—to show in more detail how relocation services work at these institutions and the strengths and weaknesses of this approach to assisting dual-career couples.

Relocation services are fairly common in the for-profit sector, where it is estimated that thousands of families move every year. Recent figures show that 65 percent of people in the workforce are in dual-career relationships (Uhland 1999). According to Eby and Allen (1998), the cost of relocating to a new city has been estimated at about $45,000 per homeowning family. In addition to the financial costs of moving, most companies recognize the human costs and offer some sort of assistance to help employees and their families cope with the social and psychological stresses of moving (Eby and Allen 1998). Many families find that their standard of living decreases after a move (Uhland 1999). These are significant obstacles that may discourage couples from moving.

Several types of relocation assistance are common in business and industry and cover a range of benefits: company-paid visits to the new area, cultural information, real-estate assistance, spouse or partner employment assistance, information about care for children or older relatives, educational information, cost-of-living adjustments, and help in selling the current home (Eby and Allen 1998). There is little empirical research examining the specific relation between relocation assistance and adjustment, but most anecdotal accounts clearly support the importance of all of these types of help.

Relocation Services in Higher Education

Although colleges and universities share some relocation concerns with businesses and government organizations such as the State Department and the military, the characteristics of the labor market are unique to each sector. For example, individuals usually voluntarily apply for positions in colleges and universities, whereas in the business and military sectors relocating or staying put may not always be up to the worker. Also, college and university employees typically do not move as frequently as is common in some businesses.

Perhaps for these reasons, colleges and universities have paid comparatively little attention to the relocation needs of faculty and administrative staff. Although some effort may be made for top-level administrators, meeting the relocation needs of faculty and their spouses is less prevalent and less systematic. Faculty hiring in general is decentralized, and efforts to help dual-career couples find suitable employment are often ad hoc. Informal services for spouses or partners depend on whether department chairs or colleagues have the willingness and knowledge to provide relocation information and to help by sending vitae or providing the names of potential employers in the community. Spouses or partners are then expected to make contacts on their own. Such help is ad hoc in that it may or may not be provided to all new hires. If one is lucky enough to be offered a faculty position in a department where the chair and colleagues recognize its importance, have many contacts, and have the time, the accompanying partner may get some help in finding a job. In less fortunate circumstances, prospective faculty may not receive the same kinds of assistance.

Formal relocation services, as described in this chapter, provide a range of community information to all initial hires and help the accompanying spouse or partner find suitable employment. What distinguishes formal services is that the college or university supports them with a budget and even a full- or part-time coordinator and they are theoretically available to all prospective employees.

There are no definitive data on the prevalence and extent of either formal or informal relocation services in higher education. In 1997 Raabe reported that 44 percent of the respondents to her national survey said they provided some sort of job assistance for spouses. An additional 12 percent said they were planning to implement such a job assistance policy.

In our own national survey of members of the Association of American

Colleges and Universities, discussed in chapter 2, over half (53 percent) of the institutions with policies and 49 percent of those without them said they provide some help to couples. Helping a spouse or partner adjust to a new community and find employment outside or inside the university takes a number of forms, from passive assistance (providing information), to somewhat more active assistance (sending résumés or helping to write résumés) to very active involvement through dual-career relocation offices. Among the AAC&U institutions responding to our survey, the most common approaches fall into the middle category. Provosts typically reported sending vitae and providing contacts inside and outside the institution (see chapter 2). Institutions both with and without formal policies are likely to provide these somewhat active forms of assistance for spouses and partners seeking faculty as well as nonfaculty positions. We conclude, based on our survey data, that most colleges and universities provide information but place the onus for making contacts on new faculty members and their spouses or partners.

Offering Formal Relocation Assistance to Dual-Career Couples

Colleges and universities in our study that had spouse or partner assistance policies typically used more active approaches, particularly for those seeking employment outside the university. The most common approach to helping spouses or partners find positions outside the university was to send letters or make phone calls on their behalf. Twenty-five of the institutions that responded to our survey said they used institutional networks and connections. In the words of one of our respondents, "We do all in our power to try to introduce the trailing spouse to local businesses/community colleges, etc." Formal relocation services are becoming more prevalent, particularly in large universities. Not only are some universities recognizing the competitive advantage relocation services offer, but they are also beginning to understand that if they are to retain faculty, the spouse or partner has to be happy as well.

Forms of Assistance

Relocation offices may provide a coordinator to offer services such as job counseling, résumé advice, or job listings; send information such as position announcements and classified advertisements to the spouse or partner; and pay for the accompanying spouse to visit campus. Several institutions in our survey reported setting up formal consortia to assist dual-career couples. In fact, almost by definition, most relocation offices participate in some kind of network of local employers. As one survey respondent stated, "We are a member of a network of local employers who communicate regularly. . . . We route résumés, set up informational interviews, and brainstorm possibilities for candidates." Another institution set up a special Area Spousal Employment Assistance Program that involved nearly one hundred businesses and universities in sharing job information for dual-career couples. Several institutions use such consortia to attract candidates.

In fall 1999, Purdue University hosted a conference of Big Ten universities specifically devoted to relocation services. That meeting revealed that most Big Ten universities have some sort of relocation services with a designated coordinator who helps, in the words of the University of Minnesota's bulletin, "new faculty, staff and their families." These offices provide information about the community and spouse or partner employment services. Purdue University, the University of Iowa, Pennsylvania State University, the University of Nebraska, the University of Arkansas, Texas A&M University, and the University of California, Santa Cruz, are some of the universities we could identify as having officially designated programs to assist dual-career couples.

Common Characteristics of Relocation Services

A review of these programs' brochures reveals several common characteristics. First, they serve new employees and those in the recruitment process for one year or in some cases up to two years. Second, they all have formal program brochures describing the services they offer. Although the brochures differ in glossiness, the mere existence of published materials signifies the university's commitment to the program and makes it available to all new eligible employees. Third, all these formal programs include in their published materials a statement releasing the program from legal responsibility for finding the spouse or partner a job. The University of Arkansas's pamphlet states, "The Dual-Career Employment Network will make every effort to provide available employment information to individuals who qualify for assistance. However, the Family Employment Program does not guarantee employment for partners of new employees."

As we shall see in the case studies reported later, this is one of the most difficult aspects of providing relocation services. Although all universities that provide such services include a disclaimer releasing the university or relocation office from the obligation to find a client a job, the employee and partner frequently interpret the offer of assistance as a contract. Fourth, all of these programs have a specifically identified program coordinator who is employed full time or at least half time by the university to provide relocation services. Most programs also have some secretarial support.

Differences among Programs

There are some important differences among programs. For example, the programs identified through our study, the Purdue Conference, and Web sites differ in their reporting structures. To preserve the anonymity of our case study sites, we will not identify specific university reporting structures here but will describe them in general terms. Most of the programs report to or are a part of a university's human resources unit. In some cases the relocation program reports to an academic administrator such as the vice provost or dean of the faculties. One university's dual-career program is located in the Office of Human Resources but is jointly sponsored by the dean of faculties and the office of human resources. In yet another case, the office is part of the human relations unit, which includes affirmative action.

Programs also differ slightly in the services offered and in who is eligible for them. The most inclusive programs serve new faculty members, professional and administrative staff, civil service staff, and classified staff or union members. Other programs specify faculty and senior administrators. Typically, universities that restrict eligibility do so because they lack sufficient staff to accommodate a larger caseload, not because they do not believe other groups need assistance. Generally speaking, relocation and dual-career offices tend to serve spouses and partners seeking employment off campus rather than on campus. Nonetheless, many of the programs we have seen help those seeking on-campus employment as well. The timing of when an accompanying spouse or partner can take advantage of relocation services also varies across institutions. As is evident in the following two case studies, at some institutions the services are offered to all finalists in a search so that a couple can make the likelihood of employment for the accompanying spouse a factor in deciding whether to come to the university. In other cases the complete services of the office are granted only to partners of faculty who have accepted a position at the institution. The couple thus has to take it on faith that the search attempt will succeed.

There are two dimensions to the services offered: the breadth of service and the activity of the relocation specialist. Most programs offer a full range of job-seeking services, from counseling to assistance with writing résumés and cover letters to contacts with employers. Programs differ in the degree to which the relocation or dual-career program makes contacts for spouses and partners. Some programs provide lists of prospective employers and leave the rest up to the spouse or partner. Other programs will actually contact potential employers. One important service some programs provide is a letter of introduction from the dual-career/relocation assistance coordinator. Programs can either focus on specific services designed to help the spouse or partner find employment or provide more extensive relocation information concerning housing, schools, day care, and such. One cannot always tell by the name of the program (relocation or dual-career office) the extent to which the program provides general information or assistance with relocation.

Some universities have organized career networks with other universities and employers in the area, where job information and names of prospective employees are shared both ways. The University of Arkansas has just such a network. It defines a dual-career employment network as a "partnership of area employers providing employment assistance for dual-career families' relocation to the region" (McLoud 2001). The University of California, Santa Cruz, helped to create the Bay Area Higher Education Recruitment Consortium, a collaborative effort of Bay Area colleges and universities (Aebersold 2001). The University of Iowa and Purdue University also belong to career networks. In fact, most universities that have relocation offices participate in informal, if not formal, career networks with local businesses and industries. These universities share recruiting information and resources. The purpose of such networks is both to "inform the community of the availability of talented professionals and to relay available employment opportunities to relocating partners" (McLoud 2001). To be successful, career networks at a minimum need financial support, a coordinator, and actively maintained professional affiliations with groups such as hospitals, school districts, and chambers of commerce. Such collaborative efforts may provide unintended benefits to the host university and to the local business community. Both cases described below demonstrate how participation in these types of networks, formal or informal, can be very beneficial in creating positive town-gown relations.

University relocation programs are relatively new and therefore either have not completed evaluations or have not published the results of their evaluations. The information that does exist suggests that client satisfaction is very high. The University of California, Santa Cruz, has published the results of its program evaluation. Although the service is only a year old, all parties who had used it were very satisfied. This included deans, department chairs, and hiring officials: 70 percent reported that the service had helped them recruit and retain faculty and staff (Aebersold 2001). Likewise, the University of Arkansas network has reported placing an average of 60 percent of referrals between 1998 and 2001 (P. McLoud, personal communication, 2001). The two institutions we highlight in this chapter have done evaluations of their respective programs, and this information will be woven into our discussion.

Relocation/dual-career assistance is an important and significant service that colleges and universities can provide for faculty and staff. In fact, relocation services are potentially less controversial than some of the other options for dealing with the dual-career employment needs of today's faculty. In this chapter we focus on case studies of two universities to illustrate in greater depth the types of relocation programs that exist and the services they offer.

Relocation Assistance at Heartland University

"Heartland University's" dual-career program provides assistance to all new faculty spouses or partners seeking employment and is the formal way Heartland helps spouses or partners find nonteaching positions both in and outside the university. (See chapter 3 for fuller description of "Heartland University.") As part of its effort to bolster faculty recruiting, in 1993 Heartland hired a half-time dual-career coordinator who reports to the associate vice chancellor for academic affairs. Heartland understands that responding to family and work tensions is an important part of its effort to recruit high-quality faculty to its small midwestern city. As stated in the policy document, "The emphasis of the Dual-Career Program will be on assisting in the development of employment opportunities for the professional partners of faculty and administrators when the partner is new to the community." The program specifically applies to partners who are new to the community and not to those who have lived there for a while. This restriction was imposed because of limited staff time and resources. The dual-career coordinator at the time we visited had a master's degree in industrial psychology and was a half-time appointment.

The program works as follows. Candidates in all faculty and administrative searches are informed about the dual-career program through a brochure included in a packet of material given to each candidate before the on-campus interview. As stated in the program policy document, "This mechanism provides a way to inform candidates (beyond the advertisement statement) that the University has a proactive policy concerning dual-career couples and that it is appropriate to discuss such concerns with department chairs and deans with whom the candidate interviews." Informing, or attempting to inform, candidates of the existence of the office and program at the interview stage serves two important functions. First, it alerts potential faculty and administrators that they can raise the issue of spouse and partner employment during their campus visit. Second, it "help[s] candidates and their partners determine their employment possibilities prior to a formal offer being extended" (Rathert 2001). Although such knowledge could discourage potential candidates, awareness should be a part of relocation preparation and can also reduce the stress associated with relocating a family (Martin 1999).

When a job candidate's partner or spouse contacts the Dual-Career Office, usually by sending a vita, the coordinator interviews the person with the goal of developing an individualized job-search strategy. Some of the typical forms of assistance include "(1) letters of introduction to local employers, (2) networking connections, (3) referrals from the coordinator regarding local position openings, (4) moral support, and (5) resume/cover letter advice" (Rathert 2001). The office also helps arrange interviews if necessary. The partner or spouse may use the services of the Dual-Career Office for up to one year after relocating to Heartland City.

A big part of the dual-career coordinator's job is establishing ongoing relationships with local businesses and agencies that are potential employers. In fact, most of the partners and spouses who use the Dual-Career Office's services are placed in the community. Approximately 120 nonuniversity to 40 university positions have been filled through this office since 1992. Heartland's relocation program has been very successful. In fact, it has been so successful that, in the words of the dual-career coordinator, some area businesses "have had to expand because they have found talented people that could begin programs they had wanted to start." One of the unintended positive effects of Heartland's program is precisely that the dual-career coordinator establishes "concentric circles of relations" among the university, local employers, and the Dual-Career Office.

Perceived Strengths and Weaknesses of Heartland's Program

Heartland recently conducted an evaluation of the program that sheds some light on how it works and how well it encourages families to accept positions at Heartland and to stay there. Approximately 120 couples used the service between 1994 and 1999. These couples knew about the program from the start but were split on whether it had played a part in the decision to accept a position at Heartland and whether it helped the accompanying spouse or partner find a job. When the man was the original hire, couples seemed to be more satisfied with the dual-career program than when the woman was the original hire (Rathert 2001). This finding is not surprising; some research suggests that being an accompanying spouse or partner is harder on a man because of societal expectations about men's role as the chief breadwinner (Hendershott 1995).

From the perspective of the original hire and the accompanying spouse, each case is unique, so it is difficult to identify a common pattern across the interviews. Nonetheless, one woman described her journey:

> We arrived here in 1995 and [my husband] had a position lined up. That's the reason we came here. Originally, I didn't think there'd be a problem finding a job here. I figured I'd be able to get something on campus or perhaps in the school district because I'd also been a high school principal. But when I got here I realized that things are very tight. . . . I interviewed with a number of people on campus and part of . . . the great thing about this university is that when they interview a person for a position, they invite the spouse to come along. They provide a rental car for the spouse, set up a series of interviews on and off campus, depending on what you're interested in. And the dual-career program person works with the administrative assistant and vice chancellor's office to set up the whole itinerary. That hadn't happened before in my experience.

The current coordinator of the Dual-Career Office noted that even in the short time she had been on the job, "A couple of partners have said, 'My wife chose to come here largely because of this program. This had a lot to do with our decision to come here.'" Deans reiterated the idea that they had been able to hire people they might not otherwise have attracted: "I think we have made some very good hires that we could never have made otherwise. . . . It is not easy for couples to move. If we can look at couples and think about hiring couples, oftentimes we can find a very interesting fit. That is a good thing for us. . . . It's good for retention."

From the faculty member's perspective, the program and especially the services of the Dual-Career Office demonstrated a level of concern and interest in the partner not frequently seen. One dean commented, "Occasionally I have a candidate say they were pleased that they were already contacted by the Dual-Career Office and that there seemed to be a real interest in their situation."

We found very few negative perceptions of the services offered by the Dual-Career Office. However, this might be because we did not interview people who had used the services to find work outside the university. When we originally selected Heartland as a case study site, we were unaware that it offered relocation services. As such, we had not arranged a large number of interviews to explore this aspect of its dual-career accommodation policy. That said, based on the faculty and administrators we did interview and the data from the institution's own program evaluation, we conclude that there are few downsides to operating a relocation office like Heartland's. The success of Heartland's program (and other programs that offer similar services) is somewhat dependent on the larger economy and the availability of work. Spouses and partners who are forced to settle for lower-paying work or to take less than perfect jobs may be less satisfied with services. Such problems, however, are beyond the control of relocation offices.

Relocation Assistance at Riverdale University

"Riverdale University" also has a well-developed program to assist dual-career couples, the Spousal Relocation Assistance Program (SRAP). (See chapter 3 for fuller description of "Riverdale University.") SRAP primarily serves spouses seeking employment in nonfaculty posts, both inside and outside the university. Although in practice Riverdale may accommodate unmarried couples—either heterosexual or gay and lesbian—the policy explicitly uses the word spouse.

SRAP is both elaborate in the services offered and straightforward in the way it works. The program has an office and what started as a half-time relocation specialist. The position has now become full time. The relocation specialist shares a secretary with other offices in her building. When we visited, Shari, the relocation specialist, also had a student working in the office. Shari holds a doctorate in counseling psychology. Organizationally, the relocation office is one area under the charge of the vice president for human relations. The vice president is also responsible for the affirmative action office and offices that address gender and racial diversity on campus. When we asked why Riverdale developed SRAP, the coordinator replied, "I think we had a particularly foresightful vice president who worked very hard at women's issues." The office has been in existence for eight or nine years.

The acting vice president for human relations explained why it is important for Riverdale to help faculty spouses:

> Most women faculty, I think the numbers bear this out, are part of dual-career couples, and the same is true for minority faculty. It is becoming true for faculty in general. That is the reality where universities find themselves. Faculty in particular, the same is true for administrative staff, are increasingly in dual-career families. If we are going to attract those talented individuals to the university, then we are aided if we can some way assist the trailing spouse. . . . I was a trailing spouse when we came to Riverdale. My husband was on the faculty in clinical psychology. I had a law career and there was no assistance for us. There were mild efforts. . . . I commuted to ——. . . . There was no . . . assistance for faculty. That has changed, and I am glad that it has changed in eleven years. We recognize that trailing or accompanying spouses make decisions about their career if they make a move to support their spouse or partner's career. People are not going to give it up. Some are. But we find that the bulk want to maintain an active career. And if you are going to retain faculty long term, you have to make a decision in the short term. . . . I think the university recognizes that. We are at somewhat of a disadvantage because of our physical location, which means that we need to have that [assistance].

SRAP is well entrenched at Riverdale, and it functions in a straightforward and relatively automatic way. The program has very nice, professionally designed brochures, and when a search committee is formed the affirmative action officer is notified and informs SRAP. The SRAP office immediately mails the search committee chair an administrator's packet containing information about use of the program, the community, and the services offered by SRAP, as well as several copies of general relocation packets. Packets are to be given to the top three candidates, and those invited for on-campus interviews may schedule appointments with the relocation specialist. Once candidates have accepted a position and indicated they want SRAP services, and once the department chair or search committee chair has authorized such services, the spouse can become an official client. Shari has another packet of materials for the accompanying spouse. So in order to benefit from SRAP services, the original hire has to have accepted a position at Riverdale. Couples have to have faith that the accompanying spouse will eventually get a job. Shari explained the rationale for this:

> Very often when new recruits come they say, "We're not coming unless we have jobs for both of us." We can't deliver that. They [jobs] just can't be delivered on

a half-time position in a small town. . . . What we can do to solve that problem—two things. One, I can work with them for a long time and I'm pretty relentless and pretty successful. And the second thing is that we offer businesses reciprocal service. That has been significant and key. So if, for example, a new faculty member has a wife that is good in metals, has some degree in metals, if —— would agree to speak to this person . . . then I am also free to help their incoming spouse for free. That has really been key.

The SRAP specialist provides couples with very detailed information about the area and job opportunities, employment trends, and more personal individual needs that people have when they move to a new place. Shari explained the initial steps she takes:

We review the spouse's résumé for possible editing, reformatting; a Client Pool Web site paragraph will be prepared; any needed career testing will be scheduled; responses to job interview questions are prepared in advance, etc. These preliminary tasks are completed as quickly as possible so that the spouse will be ready for active job searching. The relocation specialist begins to research and prepare a customized start-up networking list. Frequent contact between the spousal client and the relocation specialist is initiated and maintained for the duration of services and may last up to one year.

Shari, Riverdale's relocation specialist, actually provides much broader services. As a longtime resident of the area, she was credited by those we interviewed with providing important information on everything from where African American women can get their hair done to doctors and schools. She keeps detailed records on her contacts with her clients; and although she is supposed to work with them for only one year, she keeps them on longer if necessary. As she explained, there are two possible outcomes for a client: employment or a "decision." A decision might be to return to school or to stay at home and not seek employment. In either case, SRAP considers a decision to be a successful outcome.

It became clear from speaking with the relocation specialists at both Riverdale and Heartland that relocation is a far more emotional experience for the accompanying spouse than we had imagined. Consequently the relocation coordinator must be prepared to offer counseling services beyond merely providing information and contacts. As Shari noted, "Spouses are sometimes an entirely different population than new hires. New hires are often excited about their new appointments and are eager to get started. Some of them have to hit the ground running, so to speak, and positive things start happening quickly. Not all the spouses and partners are quite as happy or enthusiastic as the new hire." For example, one spouse had told Shari, "My husband insists that I work, but I am too sick to work." She asked Shari, "[Will you] act like you are job-searching for me but not really do it?" Shari described another client who doesn't intend to move to Riverdale but hasn't yet told the spouse (the new hire). These kinds of situations suggest that hiring new faculty members is often far more complicated than most hiring committees ever know. Fortunately, these situations are the exception. The relocation specialists we spoke with vary in how much they encourage personal counseling, but institutions contemplating providing relocation services should be aware that some complex ethical and personal issues may arise that require the attention of staff with appropriate qualifications.

SRAP also provides "reciprocal services" to spouses or partners of employees of area businesses that cooperate with Riverdale in hiring. Shari maintains careful records documenting how many clients she has had and how many have arrived at a decision, which is somewhat reassuring to couples. As she noted, "We just keep widening the network circles until we get what we want." Since 1999, SRAP has had 228 university and 20 reciprocal clients. The office has provided services to 142 additional spouses or partners that did not become clients. Of the 248 official clients, 81 found jobs, 43 reached a decision, and 76 remain active clients. Approximately three-quarters of the clients have been female, except during the 1999 academic year, when the gender distribution was about equal. Additionally, although the percentage has varied from year to year, faculty spouses constitute the majority of clients.

Perceived Strengths and Weaknesses of Riverdale's Approach

There were few complaints about SRAP and much praise. From the institutional point of view its strengths are that, if not actually instrumental in a faculty's member's decision to accept a position at Riverdale, it is credited with being helpful in decision making. As the acting vice president of human relations explained, "So that the actual decision to come or not come, I don't know that the relocation program has much to do with that initially. . . . I think it is supportive of them in that crucial period between accepting the offer and actually arriving and getting going with one's career. . . . An accommodation program may be more important for couples in which both are academics."

The downside for the institution is that the program has been too success-ful. It has outgrown the capacity of one half-time relocation specialist. There were some complaints, though relatively few, because the services of SRAP are made available only after the initial hire has accepted a position. Depart-ment chairs told about losing faculty because the spouse failed to find em-ployment in the Riverdale area, but that was at least in part because of the na-ture of the accompanying spouse's work rather because SRAP failed.

Although not all the accompanying spouses we spoke with were entirely happy with their current employment situation, they had very positive things to say about Shari and the services she offers through SRAP. She had pro-vided leads on jobs, given information on how the Riverdale University per-sonnel system worked, offered hints about conducting a job search, given in-formation about the job market, passed on phone numbers of employers, provided letters from SRAP, and offered constant follow-up. Finding a desir-able job sometimes took time, and accompanying spouses were not always totally satisfied. As Loeb (1997) noted in her study of a similar program at the University of Illinois, accompanying spouses or partners often must accept work that is not ideal and may be of significantly lower quality than that of-fered their partners. Nevertheless, most former clients spoke very positively about the service. One woman seemed to speak for all who had been assisted via SRAP when she said:

> I felt really comforted by it in the fact that there was at least somebody I knew that was working on my side and somebody that I felt comfortable going to. We talked to one another probably two or three times a week. . . . For me, four months is a while not to be working. . . . [SRAP services] was a little stress relief because I had moved across the country and it was enough just getting accli-mated to the area, but then to have somebody who I had even been talking with before I moved out here who said, "Don't worry about it. You'll find something. Just be patient. Something will come along." It was nice to know that somebody within the university system could kind of guide me along the way.

If there were complaints about SRAP it was that communication should be better. Even though SRAP is a formal office with a budget and nice bro-chures, there were still glitches in ensuring that all new hires and their spouses were informed about the program. Not all had been told about it by the department heads or their husbands (or wives). Despite this assertion by some, very few changes were even suggested by those we interviewed.

Budgetary Considerations

We did not collect specific budgetary information on each program, but we can estimate costs based on staffing levels. Staff salaries are the biggest component of the relocation services budget. Heartland had a half-time professional position with half-time secretarial support. Riverdale also had a half-time specialist (the position has since become full time), secretarial support, and occasional assistance from a graduate assistant. Operating budgets include the typical expenses such as phone, fax, postage, and office supplies. They also include money for publications and Web site development. Riverdale had sophisticated, multicolor publications, while Heartland's were much simpler. As Riverdale's relocation specialist pointed out, the program must have office space with enough privacy for confidential conversations. She estimated that the cost per client runs about $1,300, which is easily less than it costs to conduct a national search should a faculty member leave. The goodwill resulting from this investment is not easily quantified.

Concluding Comment

Although a small percentage of faculty hired have spouses or partners who seek tenure-track faculty lines within the same university, a greater percentage seek employment in nonfaculty roles, either within or outside the college or university. Formal relocation offices or services of the type described here can greatly ease the job hunt specifically and the transition to a new community more generally. Although there is little empirical evidence, there is some reason to believe that formal relocation services may help universities compete for faculty and establish positive relationships with their surrounding communities.

It is clear from our case study sites that with the assistance of the relocation coordinators, accompanying spouses and partners are likely to find suitable employment either on campus or in the local community. In assisting those searching for on-campus administrative positions, the relocation specialist can help an accompanying spouse or partner negotiate the interinstitutional bureaucracy, can assist in contacts and make introductions to those who have positions within the institution, can serve as a clearinghouse for on-campus employment opportunities, and can counsel accompanying spouses or partners to think broadly about their skills and interests. These services are helpful to those with terminal degrees who cannot find a suitable academic position nearby and who are willing to think broadly about their interests and skills. Certainly, trends within student services toward a more academic focus and toward improved cooperation with academic departments will help those with academic backgrounds and credentials who are searching for administrative positions. In addition, relocation services are ideal for helping accompanying spouses or partners find work in the community outside the college or university. In this regard, the coordinators of the programs at Heartland and Riverdale both cited positive relations with local businesses and industries as an unintended outcome of their relocation programs.

5 | Accommodation through Non-Tenure-Track and Adjunct Faculty Positions

Although she had just completed her Ph.D. in biology, Ann was considered by many to be a rising star in her field. She had received offers of employment from two excellent state institutions before accepting a position at Belle State University.

Ann and her husband, Steve, considered a number of factors before Ann decided to accept this job offer. Belle State was well regarded, paid reasonably well, and had all the resources she needed to pursue her scholarship. Ann also had an immediate rapport with the faculty, and she sensed that the students were unusually academically oriented. As a land grant university, the institution was strong in the sciences, and Ann felt confident that she would get the start-up resources she needed.

In addition to factors related to her professional life, Ann also took into account more personal concerns. She had some family living not far from Belle State, and she would welcome their support. She also liked the city where her new job would be located—especially its reputation for having an excellent public school system. Their only child would be starting kindergarten in a year, and Ann and Steve agreed that her education should be a high priority. Steve figured prominently in Ann's decision in another way: they both thought he would have better employment opportunities if Ann signed on with this school rather than with the other institution that had offered her a position.

Steve too had just finished a Ph.D.—in sociology. Because there were so many recent doctoral graduates in that discipline, Steve had been unable to find a satisfactory job, let alone one at an institution where Ann could also work. Although Belle State did not offer Steve a tenure-track job, it did offer him a three-quarter-time appointment for at least two years, with the possibility for renewal. Ann and Steve hoped that a tenure-track position in sociology would open up soon, but at least they would both be working at the same institution for the next two years, during which they could continue to assess their options and plan for the future.

Finding a nonpermanent, non-tenure-track, or part-time faculty position for an accompanying spouse or partner is the most common approach to accommodating dual-career academic couples. This approach has been adopted by institutions with formal dual-career policies as well as by those without them. Such accommodations are easiest at larger comprehensive and research universities because temporary full-time faculty lecturers, instructors, or visiting professors, as they are variously called, are fairly numerous at these institutions (Baldwin and Chronister 2001). These positions exist at smaller liberal arts colleges as well, although such hires may be more difficult to accommodate owing to institutional size and limited resources. Part of the popularity of this approach to accommodating dual-career academic couples comes from the growing reliance on adjunct positions in general. By some estimates, more than 40 percent of the faculty in higher education work in part-time positions. The National Center for Education Statistics also reports (NCES 2002) that over 26 percent of full-time faculty are at the rank of instructor or lecturer and are thus not on the tenure track. These figures have risen significantly over the past twenty years, and by all indications they will continue to do so. These data are supported by figures from the American Association of University Professors (AAUP), which reports that more than half of all faculty appointments are currently in non-tenure-track positions. As a growing proportion of faculty hires are in part-time and non-tenure-track positions, it makes sense that hiring an accompanying spouse or partner into a temporary position would be a popular means of making a dual-career accommodation.

Although only 38 percent of the chief academic officers who responded to our survey (38 percent with a spouse or partner accommodation policy and 16 percent without) said they would "create a non-tenure-track position" to accommodate a dual-career couple, we suspect these figures actually underestimate the extent to which temporary faculty positions are an option for accompanying spouses and partners. This is because such positions may already exist and need not be specially created.

In response to the open-ended question in our survey asking about typical accommodations, thirty-nine respondents described hiring an accompanying spouse or partner in a non-tenure-track appointment. Some of these partners were hired to teach part time, some were hired as sabbatical replacements, others received research associate positions, and still others were granted full-time adjunct or instructor positions. In their descriptions of these hires, most provosts noted that there was really no such thing as a "typical" accommodation, since the couples' needs and the institutions' opportunities are idiosyncratic. A characteristic response to this question comes from a provost at a selective liberal arts college who described a scenario where their first-choice candidate for a position requested work for her spouse. The institution, in response, arranged for him to teach two courses per semester. At a research institution, a provost explained that in their only successful case of accommodating a dual-career couple, the accompanying spouse was hired to fill an already available temporary position. The provost noted that his office did not "interfere with the selection process." A twist on this form of accommodation is to offer spouses or partners "courtesy appointments" in which the accompanying partner receives no monetary compensation but is allowed access to such university perquisites as the library, computer and Internet access, and office space. One of the benefits of such an appointment is that it typically allows incumbents to apply for research grants to support themselves with soft money in lieu of a earning a university salary.

Because of the extensive use of non-tenure-track faculty in higher education, the characteristics of such positions and how they are established and filled are as individual as their institutions and units. In this chapter we describe two institutions that have different approaches to using non-tenure-track faculty positions to accommodate spouses or partners of sought-after faculty members. In the case of Belle State, non-tenure-track positions are an ad hoc solution. The university has no formal dual-career hiring policy. Heartland, on the other hand, has a university-wide policy and procedure for creating temporary, non-tenure-track positions for spouses and partners.

The Belle State Experience

"Belle State University" is one institution that, while lacking a formal written policy, accommodates at least some accompanying spouses and partners by providing limited-term visiting appointments. (See chapter 3 for fuller description of "Belle State University.") Belle State has on occasion also created tenure-track positions for spouses or partners, but the vast majority of its accommodations are through visiting appointments. These appointments may be funded in part by the Provost's Office. A request for an accommodation is most frequently made when a department is trying to hire an extremely desirable faculty member who has an academic spouse. As one member of the Provost's Office explained, "The University needs to do everything they can to attract the very best faculty. . . . The driving force is almost always the primary hire. That person is somebody that a department wants and is an out-standing person and people are saying essentially that we are going to do what it takes to try to hire that person. To not do that is just plain stupid."

Representatives of the Provost's Office stressed repeatedly that depart-ments are never pressured to appoint an accompanying spouse or partner. As one member of the office commented: "We would not tell any department to hire someone just because they happened to be married to somebody we wanted to hire. We obviously can't to that. . . . It's not very pleasant to stick someone in somewhere and faculty not want to have them."

When the Provost's Office is asked to get involved, either a department chair or a dean will make the initial inquiry. Most times it is a dean who calls because, as both the assistant provost for equal opportunity and the interim provost explained, taking requests from department chairs or associate deans may result in a conflict. In the words of the interim provost, "You don't know if the dean or whoever is the head of the unit is in agreement." In fact, when department chairs approach the Provost's Office about money for a visiting appointment or other form of accommodation assistance, they are told to ask the appropriate dean, who must be in agreement and who might be able to solve the problem at the unit level, so that the provost need not get involved. In fact, when spouses or partners are in the same college, the col-lege typically handles the matter internally and with the assistant provost for equal opportunity. In these cases the Provost's Office may not even know of the accommodations. Indeed, this is one of the problems in tracking their prevalence. Cross-college appointments require deans to contact other deans. Because they essentially involve asking one dean to give up a portion of the salary budget to help another unit hire a sought-after faculty member, it is here that the Provost's Office is most likely to be asked for money.

If a department decides to consider hiring a spouse or partner as a visiting professor, it typically interviews that person like a regular applicant. This step not only helps to ensure a reasonably good fit between the department and the visiting faculty member but also helps to satisfy affirmative action re-quirements. The assistant provost for equal opportunity explains:

> We approve those [visiting] positions, and one of our basic requirements is that the person has to meet all of the job qualifications were you to advertise for the position. That's just a basic for anything. What we are doing is waiving the for-mal search process in this case, and this is one of those exceptions we make to effect a hire in the department. . . . So that is really our basic requirement, that

this has to be a really viable candidate that could be strong if we were to do a search and they were to apply for this position outright.

While no department *has* to accommodate an accompanying spouse, the Provost's Office makes it attractive to do so by partially funding the spouse's position if asked. As one interviewee remarked, "I can't imagine any department turning down the fact that the Provost's Office would fund a position."

Faculty who are initially hired as visiting appointments can apply for tenure-track positions when they become available, and in some cases it is thought that they have an advantage over other applicants. A spokesperson in the Provost's Office reported that "if they were doing a good job, they'd probably have the inside track." According to this spokesperson, "A number of [visiting faculty do apply for tenure-track positions]. And in fact, there are people who enter the university that way." Even if a short-term appointment does not eventually lead to a regular tenure-track position, representatives of the Provost's Office believe that such appointments at least help spouses or partners of regular hires to familiarize themselves with the professional alternatives that exist in the area.

Perceived Strengths of Visiting, Non-Tenure-Track Positions at Belle State

Visiting, non-tenure-track positions offer several benefits to the institution as a means of accommodating spouses and partners. First, it is quite a bit easier to hire an accompanying spouse or partner into a visiting position than to create a new tenure-track position or commit an existing position for that purpose. And from the faculty point of view, making visiting appointments does not draw the antagonism that creating tenure-track positions often attracts. The interim provost at Belle State felt strongly that neither he nor anyone else could tell a department to "hire somebody just because they happened to be married to somebody we wanted to hire." In his words, "That's why the visiting appointment is much more convenient, because it gives that faculty a chance to meet and look at the individual and then make a decision and give this person a chance to just be in the area and find something that might be better." So from this perspective the adjunct or visiting appointment is good for the department, which gets to examine the person's qualifications for a potential tenure-track position, and it is good for the individual because it gives some base for looking for something more permanent. Second, at least when visiting professors are part-time employees, their salaries will typically be relatively low, and they will probably lack health care or retirement benefits; thus these employees are less costly for the institution. Of course in-stitutions who hire full-time adjunct faculty and offer health and other ben-efits will not realize this saving (Baldwin and Chronister 2001).

Visiting appointments may also be desirable to accompanying spouses depending on their personal situations and career aspirations. Some may not want full-time positions with all the professional obligations they entail. And a visiting appointment does give a person some breathing room to look for a more permanent job. For example, the wife of a recently hired depart-ment chair found a one-year full-time appointment that fit her needs per-fectly. When the husband, the initial hire, was offered the position, he re-ported being asked what it would take to get him to move to Belle State. He replied that he would like a job for his wife. His wife had been a community college librarian for twenty-eight years. The dean of the husband's college contacted the head of libraries who created a job for which the wife was qual-ified. The position was for one year only, but both understood that there was a chance the wife could stay on depending on the needs of the library. This commitment was sufficient for the husband to accept Belle State's offer. For the wife, "It is still a one-year appointment, but that's what I really wanted. I retired from my last job, and I was happy to have that [the one-year appoint-ment]. In fact, I didn't have to have a job. I did really want to get one partly to get involved in the community, moving after so many years in one place."

Perceived Weaknesses of the Practice at Belle State

The most commonly expressed concern about Belle State's approach to ac-commodating dual-career couples is that it has not been formalized as a written policy. When asked how he would address accommodation differ-ently, one department head replied: "[There] probably should be a policy so if you do get a question you can get an answer that's reasonably straight. . . . What they [the Provost's Office] probably say is something like; 'we support spousal hiring,' which is not exactly a policy. It's a statement of intent of sup-port. What that actually means, no one knows." One faculty spouse, who had hoped for a tenure-track position but had settled for a job in academic advising, included in her reply some thoughts on the changing gender com-position of the academic labor pool:

> I think people really do need to have a spousal hiring plan now. Academics are
> no longer a bunch of single men or independent men. . . . Whatever can be done
> to make work at a university more like a full picture of life would be good. It's

not accidental that academic men marry academic women—because of their shared interests. . . . The vast majority of people that we know are in our same situation, and they are always looking for another job. Always. Someone is always planning to leave, looking for ways to leave, or leaving. . . . So I think there is a need for a policy and it should be a university-wide policy. There needs to be something in place to ensure that department heads come forward and notify the deans about a couple's job needs.

Of course, that an institution has a written policy regarding dual-career hiring will not necessarily mitigate the negative effects of some approaches to accommodation. For example, an institution may have a written policy specifying that qualified accompanying spouses may work as adjunct faculty members in certain circumstances, but adjunct positions are themselves often problematic. The need for adjunct faculty at any given college or university is variable and unstable, making it very difficult to make long-term plans. In fact, the interim provost said that Belle State was moving to making all visiting positions fixed three-year term appointments. As he said, "A decision will have to be made. You can't just hang on. We have people who have been visiting for their entire life." This move was partially motivated by new state guidelines, but people at Belle State were worried about the effect the new policy would have on the ability to use visiting positions as a means of spouse and partner accommodation.

On top of that, the pay for adjunct teaching is notoriously low. According to Baldwin and Chronister's (2001) study of nontenured faculty, the salaries for full-time non-tenure-track faculty are typically lower than for full-time tenure-track faculty with comparable experience in comparable institutional types. They also conclude, however, that most full-time non-tenure-track faculty receive benefits comparable to those of full-time tenure-track faculty. Temporary faculty also face the problem that the longer they remain in such positions the more difficult it becomes to eventually earn a tenure-track job. Several factors contribute to this, including the fact that many full-time non-tenure-track faculty carry heavier teaching loads than their tenure-track colleagues and therefore have less time for research. Further, many adjunct faculty members are treated as second-class citizens, "outsiders" who are inferior to their "real" faculty colleagues (Baldwin and Chronister 2001; Gappa 1987). This led Baldwin and Chronister to describe many such positions as being a "professional dead end" (136).

In addition, as we will see even more clearly in the case of Heartland, certain expectations that inevitably come with appointment to a visiting professorship may cause dissatisfaction. Belle State makes it clear that one has to be qualified to be a faculty member at Belle State in order to be hired in a visiting position. For example, as Belle State's assistant provost for equal opportunity noted, "[The candidate for a visiting position] has to be a viable faculty member or potential viable faculty member for a particular department." When a person is hired under these guidelines, there is often the expectation that the visiting professor will have an advantage in getting a tenure-track position, which may or may not be the case.

For example, a woman engineer whose husband had accepted a job at Belle State had been given visiting positions. Both she and her husband had earned their Ph.D.'s at Belle State. However, at the time her husband applied for his tenure-track job, the woman believed she did not have the record to merit a tenure-track position, so she did not apply. She now wonders if she might have underestimated her abilities, and she seems frustrated that although she is employed at the college in critical quasi-administrative and teaching roles, her contributions are not recognized or valued. Her newfound outlet is writing a book on women in science with several other Belle State scientists. The book is targeted to undergraduates. While this academic is making the best of her situation, she is not wholly satisfied with her status as a long-term visiting professor.

So, while Belle State does not have a formal policy for accommodating spouses or partners, its approach is probably close to that of most large research universities: hiring spouses or partners into visiting positions. This approach is relatively easy to manage in that visiting faculty generally fill a temporary need, such as when a regular faculty member is on sabbatical. In addition to meeting a real need, this approach tends not to generate antagonism from regular faculty; they know that in all likelihood the situation is short term and do not feel that their control over hiring decisions has been usurped. Hiring visiting faculty does raise some concerns, especially among those hired into these positions. They may have trouble making long-term plans, wondering how long they can *really* keep these positions and whether or not they will someday be converted into regular positions.

The Heartland Experience

"Heartland University" provides a second example of how an institution may use relatively short-term appointments to accommodate dual-career academic couples. (Refer to chapter 3 for fuller description of "Heartland University.") But unlike Belle State University, Heartland has a formal, written policy to address the employment needs of spouses and partners of recruited faculty members. Heartland's accommodation policy has two programmatic components: the Dual-Career Program described in chapter 4 and the Faculty Fellows Program. To understand the Faculty Fellows Program, it is helpful to briefly review Heartland's accommodation policy. The policy was implemented in 1992 at the suggestion of a new president who had started a similar policy at his former institution; before 1992, dual-career accommodation had been handled ad hoc. The Dual-Career Program primarily assists spouses or partners seeking employment off campus or in nonfaculty campus positions. The Faculty Fellows Program was designed to address the needs of dual-career academic couples in which both members sought faculty positions. Although Heartland City is fairly large by midwestern standards, there are relatively few higher education institutions within driving distance, and most of those are small.

The Faculty Fellows Program is designed primarily as a tool to recruit junior faculty. When a faculty member is hired into a tenure-track position, a spouse or partner who is also an academic may take advantage of the Faculty Fellows Program. This program provides spouses or partners with one-year (in most cases) appointments in teaching, research, or administration, office space, and some benefits. Faculty fellows receive a one-time stipend of $15,000, two-thirds of which is funded by the senior vice chancellor for academic affairs from a pool of money created specifically for this purpose. One-third of the funds comes from the dean hiring the accompanying spouse or partner. The hiring dean may, and often does, supplement the stipend. The fellowship is intended to be a bridge to or a place from which the individual can look for a full-time position either at Heartland or at other institutions in the area. As the dual-career policy states: "The purpose of the Fellowship is to provide the partner with support that would give the individual a base from which to seek ongoing employment, conduct research or seek external funds. The Fellowship provides opportunities for professional interaction in one's discipline and affords the person time to pursue employment in his or her field(s) either at Heartland, at neighboring institutions, or with other employers."

Typically the dean of the initial hire's college contacts the dean of the college where the accompanying spouse or partner might best fit. This is all done quite informally. Although a formal search process is not followed, the relevant departmental faculty members are usually involved to some extent in the appointment of the fellow. For example, one respondent explained, "What I do is share the vita with the faculty of the person who is the potential dual-career person, and they look at their slides and their vita. I hope they are sympathetic to it and see how this person could work in their program." Some departments have committees review adjunct or faculty fellow appointments. In almost all cases a vita is requested, and sometimes teaching evaluations and references are also requested. In many cases the individual seeking a faculty fellows appointment will be interviewed. Departments and colleges differ somewhat on attitudes toward faculty fellows and criteria for selecting them. One department that receives many requests to accommodate faculty fellow appointments considers the candidate's academic record to make sure the person is qualified for the position and tries to determine if the appointment meets a departmental need. Several other units, while employing high standards in decisions to appoint fellows, seemed almost grateful for the opportunity. These units agreed that people were seldom rejected for one-year appointments.

As we mentioned earlier, departments can supplement the $15,000 stipend or extend the accompanying spouse's or partner's contract. When they do extend a contract, however, "it is up to the deans of the colleges to continue to fund that. That is a weakness of the program. The dean has to be convinced that you, the faculty hire, are worth it so that they want to keep you and thus want to make your spouse happy. If the dean thinks you are not, then the funding falls through."

Getting more permanent appointments or being considered for tenure-track appointments is a different matter. For example, the dean of arts and sciences said, "Routinely, with few questions asked, if there is an accompanying spouse or partner, when we make a faculty hire, we do the dual-career fellowship as a minimum. I can't think of a case where it has been requested and we haven't done that in the college." Of course, as some of the participants indicated, the position was not always ideal.

For example, the experience of an assistant professor of sociology shows how awkward it is for departments even to find out if a spouse or partner needs help in finding employment:

> I interviewed here a year ago September and they offered me the job. . . . When I was here for the interview, they kept saying, "It's okay to talk about anything." They gave me this packet that had the dual-career information in it and they kept

saying, "Anything you want to talk about?" So, the last day, when it was going well and I thought I would want to work here, I said, "I notice you have a dual-career program and I am in a dual-career marriage." My husband had a one-year appointment in philosophy, non-tenure-track. They had him fax his CV. . . . He has several publications . . . but he is in a low demand field. . . . We started the dual-career program. The dual-career couple coordinator contacted him and said they have a one-year fellowship here. . . . He decided to come with me for a year to see what would happen and to take the faculty spousal fellowship.

The fellowship at Heartland was also used to attract some senior faculty and administrators. In several cases, department chairs we interviewed were also members of dual-career couples, and their spouses had been accommodated through the Faculty Fellows Program. However, there seemed to be inconsistencies in the application of the policy at this level. Some faculty and administrators at higher levels were able to obtain tenure-track positions for their spouses while others (who apparently did not insist at the time of hiring) were offered only one-year faculty fellow appointments.

Perceived Strengths of Heartland's Policy

From an institutional point of view, the Faculty Fellows Program is perceived as important. Although all administrators in charge of the policy acknowledged difficulties and were planning to make changes, respondents believe it not only assists their recruiting efforts but also is a necessary part of that effort. In the words of an acting department chair, "My view these days is that the key to successful recruiting is to always look to the partner." He continued, "As a policy issue . . . the positives are obviously a certain ethical positive of trying to do what you can to help people achieve their goals as individuals and couples. And given that there is the issue of women and minorities, I think that it is a way of achieving certain affirmative actions goals both as policy but in a more idealistic sense." One chair, in a department that receives many requests to place faculty fellows, also cited some of the benefits:

On a more pragmatic level it is a positive because it allows you to sometimes make hires of quality that you wouldn't otherwise get to make. It is also a form of predator control because if a couple has a dual-career situation, and one of them gets to be really famous, and another university tries to recruit, it's more difficult if it's a couple. People are more likely to stay if both have positions. It is a positive thing to do for the quality of the institution, and for what people believe are the goals of a university, which are to be equitable and to help people.

Several deans reiterated the idea that they had been able to hire people (for very little money) they might not otherwise have attracted: "I think we have made some very good hires that we could never have made otherwise. . . . It is not easy for couples to move. If we can look at couples and think about hiring couples, oftentimes we can find a very interesting fit. That is a good thing for us. . . . It's good for retention." A department chair in engineering noted: "The good of course is that an effort is made. Makes the spouse feel welcome, makes them feel a part of what is going on. . . . You have to do it to keep up with the competition. You have got to do it to try to get people and to be respectful of their family. It makes a better atmosphere for them. We not only want you, we want your family. That's something that is important in recruiting people."

Faculty themselves have vastly different experiences with the Faculty Fellows Program and thus have different views regarding its helpfulness. According to one administrator, "Faculty generally like the program but see difficulties." Some individuals are happy with the part-time positions, others are clearly not. An assistant professor of sociology described her thoughts: "They did more than I thought was going to be possible. We have known other people that have had less. Most of our friends haven't stayed in academia. . . . It really allowed us this year [to be together and to think about possible options]." According to another faculty member: "I think it [having a policy] is an enormous improvement over what was before, which was nothing. Not only was there nothing, but there was a terrible atmosphere; people were just not going to help you. There was no thought that there might be some useful thing for the university to do to help retain these faculty and to utilize these faculty." A woman who ended up in student affairs, who was treated as if she were eligible for the Faculty Fellows Program even though she technically was not, was quite satisfied with both the services provided and the outcomes:

> [During my husband's interview] the department chair turned my name in to the Dual-Career Office, and Kathy contacted me, which I thought was really nice, instead of me having to contact them. She interviewed me in terms of what my expectations were, asked me to send her a copy of my résumé . . . she gave me an idea of what she would try to do in terms of sending my résumé out to the various departments on campus and within the community. . . . I was very attractive

to them [the department] because the dual-career program pays two-thirds of my salary and he [vice chancellor] only had to pay one-third. . . . I thought that was really nice that they set me up with contacts. . . . I really like that Kathy initiated everything, started the contacts . . . it was nice to have somebody somewhere who could at least get the ball rolling. She was also very informative about schools for the kids, places to live. It was more than just job opportunities. . . . I appreciated the continual feedback she gave me throughout the year too.

In some cases the faculty fellowship also helped accompanying spouses obtain permanent employment. In the words of one respondent, "It was good to have a place to hang my hat, good to have a business card, and good to meet people here on campus. Eventually, that helped me get the position I have now."

Perceived Weaknesses of Heartland's Policy

Despite all the benefits for the university and individual faculty members, there are some serious concerns about the policy. By far the most serious problem for both the institution and individuals is that the one-year faculty fellows appointment creates false expectations that a full-time tenure-track position will be forthcoming. Despite written information that the faculty fellows appointment carries no guarantee of permanent employment, faculty we talked with whose partners had been unsuccessful in obtaining tenure-track or other more permanent positions were deeply dissatisfied. This dissatisfaction was recognized by deans and department chairs, some of whom were also members of dual-career couples who had not been accommodated as they would have liked. As an associate dean said: "If you bring people to campus for a one year thing where they get $15,000 on the hope and prayer that something will happen, unless there is something built in, I think it is almost worse than not having anything at all because it sets up expectations and you get a lot of very unhappy campers. . . . The unintended consequences can be acute unhappiness, if after that year there is no follow-through." As a department chair said, "One of the downsides of this is that when it doesn't work it leads to a lot of bitterness. People are never objective about their own spouses or partners. Not only is this person unhappy, but it has spread to the person who is a university employee."

A second area of concern was the perceived second-class status of individuals holding faculty fellow appointments. An inadvertent result of having a formal program with a name was that accompanying spouses and partners who participated in the Faculty Fellows Program were easily identified. Even when longer-term appointments were offered, "they felt like they had been defined now in a second-class role." This view stems from the commonly held notion in academe that anyone who needs help obtaining a job must be lacking in talent or effort. After all, these faculty have not prevailed in the highly competitive hiring process; their employment is a result of their spouses' success. Despite the perception, it is of course unfair to make assumptions about the qualifications of accompanying spouses. Still, the perception remains, and it can be very demoralizing.

Most deans and department chairs agreed that it was easier to find fellowship appointments within their own colleges. When they had to cross colleges, the negotiations became more difficult. Some viewed the fellowship, as the dean of the education college said, as a "chance to help out other departments, but sometimes they could care less if you get a faculty member or not." Unless a shared recognition or institutional value on hiring couples exists across campus, efforts to accommodate faculty fellows can be thwarted. It also takes time to work out intercollege appointments, and that can be a problem if one is in hot competition for a star candidate. And timing can be a problem if the Dual-Career Office doesn't, for some reason, hear soon enough so that interviews for the accompanying spouse can be arranged during the negotiation phase.

Most of the faculty we talked with had some concern about the policy. Some departments, for example, do not do a particularly good job of integrating the fellows into the department culture. Indeed, some faculty fellows reportedly were treated badly by departmental colleagues. Others were treated like any other tenure-track faculty member. Two of the most dissatisfied respondents were administrators. Presumably they had already demonstrated their value to Heartland, but Heartland had not reciprocated by finding permanent tenure-track positions for their spouses. In one case, the spouse of an administrator had interviewed for a tenure-track position but had not been selected. Another administrator whose husband had not yet found employment said she wouldn't stay at Heartland if something wasn't done for her husband. In part, the frustration and disappointment of these two women stemmed from the fact that they hadn't negotiated a permanent position for their spouses at the time they accepted their positions.

An assistant professor of sociology described what had turned out to be a less than desirable situation for her husband. He took a one-year appointment in the philosophy department at Heartland, where he felt he was not treated well. She explained: "Now he is teaching four courses a semester, driving an hour each way. He doesn't have a place, doesn't have a social life and I am working ten hours a day to make myself wanted so they will do something for him. Right now he is the top choice for a school in New York." One woman's husband had been given a longer-term appointment after she threatened to leave, but she felt he had been exploited. Another faculty member's husband was reappointed on a year-by-year contract, a continuing but not continuous appointment. After she got tenure, he was given a three-year appointment, but he still feels unappreciated. Some of what we heard at Heartland may exemplify a problem experienced fairly often by men who take jobs to support their wives' careers. Our study bears out literature from the business world suggesting that relocation is more difficult when it is the man who is the accompanying spouse or partner (Hendershott 1995).

Looking ahead at Heartland

Heartland's associate vice chancellor for academic affairs summed up the sentiments of many when she offered the opinion that "[Faculty Fellows] is a good model, and if we can get some kind of permanent funding, . . . if we could get another bigger chunk of money, [we could] at least provide some tenure-track possibilities." In fact, a committee had been formed to consider changes in the program. Although nothing definite had been decided at the time of our visit, several proposals had been placed on the table. A proposal to extend the fellowship to two to three years had been rejected because it was feared this would merely prolong false expectations. One proposal involved joint and long-range personnel planning with neighboring colleges including joint advertising for couples. The dean of arts and sciences proposed a variation of this:

> One way to honor all objectives is for the institution as a whole to identify a set of positions and to authorize appointments for a set of three times as many positions as we authorize searches for—hold some positions vacant that we are not searching for. Then when we have couples come along that fit into that broader range of institutional prioritized positions, well, we search for couples, with a view to this very broad range. So, rather than just looking for one person in arts and sciences, we look at couples who might fit into a total of three hundred positions that fit into our plan for the next five years.

A second proposal involved creating tenure-track positions that the accompanying spouse or partner could compete for. These positions would be funded by the vice chancellor for academic affairs, the primary hire's department, and the accompanying spouse's department. A third proposal involved thinking a bit differently about rank ordering candidates for positions. In this proposal, a search committee would identify all candidates who met the criteria for the position and label them as satisfactory. Then the committee would look at all the satisfactory candidates and consider such additional factors as being a member of a dual-career couple to help determine whom to hire. The administrator who suggested this recognized that this idea goes against faculty tradition. This proposal is discussed in more detail in chapter 9.

Concluding Comment

While Belle State and Heartland are both major research institutions, they differ in some respects. One major difference is that they are situated differently in relation to other universities and other employment opportunities. Because Belle State is geographically close to two other major universities, there are no doubt more opportunities for an accompanying spouse or partner with an advanced degree to find work. Heartland, in contrast, is relatively isolated, making efforts to accommodate both partners all the more critical.

A question that remains for both institutions is whether the initial faculty members they hire will remain after their spouses are no longer eligible to teach on a nontenured basis or whether their spouses or partners will feel exploited or unappreciated in their work. McNeil and Sher (1998) offer several suggestions that might be considered by all institutions that seek to accommodate spouses by hiring them in adjunct and other types of part-time positions.

> There are several possible ways to improve the status of such positions. Having longer-term contracts (even just a couple of years at a time) would help the morale of adjuncts by giving them some stability. Most institutions can make such a commitment, even if it might mean occasionally creating a new course or two. Institutional recognition (say, through opening up teaching awards to non-tenure-track instructors) would also be a low-cost way to boost adjunct morale, as would giving adjunct faculty access to institutional resources, such as career counseling. Even if formal research funding is not available, some departmental

funding for travel to conferences would help keep the adjunct involved in their field. Finally, re-entry funding, which exists on a small scale through federal funding agencies, can facilitate entry back into the post-doc market.

That both Belle State and Heartland include at least some such "benefits" for some adjuncts, yet still have morale problems among their instructors, demonstrates the limitations of this basic approach to accommodation. Yet as problematic as adjunct and other part-time, limited-term appointments can be, they are preferable to no position at all. Until institutions are able to devise more workable alternatives, they can mitigate the worst features of these positions by adopting the kinds of practices McNeil and Sher recommend.

6 | Accommodation through Split and Shared Positions

Jenny and Max were married while still in graduate school, where they both pursued degrees in American literature. Four years—and two children—later, they found themselves struggling to cope with the demands of work and family. While both Jenny and Max had found reasonably good positions right out of graduate school, they were working at institutions some two hundred miles apart. They had to maintain apartments in each of their "home" cities, commuting between them while shuffling their four-year-old son and two-year-old daughter. When Jenny discovered she was pregnant with their third child, she and Max knew something had to change. It seemed inevitable that one of them would have to give up working to be a full-time parent. But given their educational investment and genuine love of their work, they wondered whether this was really a solution. Yet for the past four years they had tried in vain to find two positions at the same institution, or even geographically close.

Jenny and Max thought they might at last have found a way to balance their professional and personal lives when they saw the job advertisement: "Tenure-track position in American literature. . . . Will consider a shared appointment." After much soul-searching, they applied for the position together. They were invited to campus for an interview. It was with both excitement and apprehension that they greeted the news that the job at Wildwood College was theirs for the taking. While the prospect of working—and living—in the same locale was almost too good to be true, the thought of managing on one salary was downright scary. And as if money worries weren't enough, Jenny and Max found themselves deeply concerned about tenure, funding for research, and benefits. Yes, the whole (growing) family would finally be together, but at what price?

When we asked the chief academic officers at AAC&U institutions to describe a "typical" accommodation, twenty provided examples of situations in which faculty members in the same academic discipline shared or split a single academic position. This approach as a response to the needs of dual-career academic couples is becoming more frequent in the sciences, most specifically in physics (McNeil and Sher 1998). And while not exclusive to liberal arts colleges, shared or split positions seem to be most common in those settings. In describing shared and split positions we draw heavily on the work of Laurie McNeil, professor of physics and astronomy at the University of North Carolina, Chapel Hill, and Marc Sher, professor of physics at the College of William and Mary. Concerned about both the problems caused by the high incidence of women physicists married to other academic scientists, specifically to other physicists, and the difficulty academic couples have in finding two tenure-track jobs, in 1998 McNeil and Sher conducted a Web-based survey of physics faculty members. The focus of the survey was academic physicists whose partners were either physicists or other scientists. They drew 620 responses to their on-line survey, and while the sample was not random, McNeil and Sher state that the demographics of respondents are representative of the population of interest. The resulting paper, along with other information for dual-career science couples, is available on the Web, and the address is listed along with other sources in appendix B.

The Varieties of "Shared" Appointments

The terms joint, split, and shared are often used interchangeably to describe positions in which two academics share a single faculty line. However, McNeil and Sher draw some distinctions between such positions. Most basically, in shared appointments a single faculty position is divided between two individuals whereas in split positions each is appointed as a half-time employee. The difference, according to McNeil and Sher, is that in a shared position both parties are considered for tenure simultaneously. In most cases, either both parties are granted tenure or neither is. Salary increases are added to the position, and the total salary is divided into two parts. In split appointments, a position is divided into two independent 0.5 FTE positions, each with a separate contract. The contract specifies that the employee will carry half a teaching, research, and advising load. Additionally, in a split position, tenure and raises are awarded separately, and each person has his or her own benefits. Theoretically there is no reason split positions have to be held by spouses. While we will use these terms as described by McNeil and Sher, we note that in looking at the existing literature and examining the responses made by provosts in our study, they are often used interchangeably, and the arrangements can take many forms.

Based on their survey of physics faculty and descriptions of scientists from other disciplines, McNeil and Sher conclude that split positions are more common than shared positions. Shared positions offer some advantages for couples not found in split positions. Specifically, in shared positions, each faculty member may have a half-time appointment or they may divide the work differently, with one partner having, say, a one-third-time appointment and the other a two-thirds appointment. In some cases two individuals sharing a position may have an appointment that amounts to more than the usual 100 percent, as when one, or both, teaches a class above the normal load or assumes an additional responsibility. In split positions too, each partner's appointment may amount to more than 50 percent, when one member of the couple, or both, teaches an extra class or takes on some other responsibility. Such variability in approach to shared and split positions was reflected in responses to our survey of provosts at AAC&U institutions. At one liberal arts college, for instance, a tenure-track faculty member in her fourth year asked to share her position with her husband (she subsequently worked two-thirds time and he one-third time). A respondent from another liberal arts college claimed that at his institution "the basic form of arrangement is converting a full position to two three-quarter positions."

To obtain more information about using shared or split positions, we conducted informal interviews with approximately fifteen academic deans at a variety of small colleges and asked them to discuss their views about such accommodations. When talking about shared positions, these deans (except for one who stated that the culture of her institution would not be supportive of faculty sharing a single position) said that they were receptive to the idea, that they had several faculty members who had been hired in split positions, and that typically it was the couple themselves who suggested this arrangement.

Tenure, Benefits, and Other Details in Shared Appointments

Tenure is one of the biggest concerns surrounding the use of shared or split positions. There are two basic ways colleges can handle the tenure and promotion process in these cases: a single tenure and promotion decision may apply to both individuals, or the two may be evaluated separately as in a formally split position. In the latter case, colleges may choose to increase the newly tenured professor's appointment to 100 percent or to leave it at its original level if one member of the couple does not earn tenure. Were one person in a shared job to leave for reasons unrelated to tenure, the institution would have to make a similar choice. If the remaining partner was untenured, it might opt to terminate him or her as well.

Retirement, health insurance, and other benefits can also be dealt with in a variety of ways. The most basic question is whether a single allotment of some or all benefits will be divided between the two partners in a shared or split position or whether each partner will receive a full, or close to full, complement of benefits that normally accrue to a full-time faculty member. The same kinds of decisions need to be made about funds for scholarly travel and research, office space, lab equipment, and merit and other raises. Some of the scientist couples in split positions cited by McNeil and Sher reported that each individual had access to all the normal perquisites associated with faculty jobs: access to grant funds, travel funds, student help, startup funds, and so on. They also reported that each partner had voting rights in faculty meetings.

As the foregoing suggests, shared and split appointments can be structured in many ways. But if there is one point respondents to our survey agreed on, it is that when such an appointment is made, it is essential that all the details, including salary, evaluation procedures, provisions for travel, research, equipment use, and such must be laid out in advance. At one institution, a couple sharing a position negotiated a "death clause" stating that if either one should die, the position would revert to the remaining spouse. They feared it would create too much emotional difficulty to lose one's spouse and one's job simultaneously. In the case of divorce, however, this same couple agreed that they would leave the institution so as not to create an uncomfortable situation for colleagues. The death and divorce clauses were explicitly spelled out in their contract. Other respondents to our survey explained that they were careful to put in writing what would happen if one member of the couple was granted tenure when the other was not. In one case the institution decided that the faculty member receiving tenure would be allowed to keep the position alone.

Verifying the credentials of both members of the couple when making the hire is viewed as especially important in the case of a shared or split position. The credentials of both must be "up to the standards" of the department at the time of their initial hire and also when it comes time for promotion. In essence, although the couple applies for the position together (couples typically write a cover letter explaining that they are a "package deal"), the department reviews their criteria individually, and both must be qualified for the position in order for the shared arrangement to be considered. When they are evaluated for tenure and promotion, both members of the couple have to meet the school's criteria. For example, institutions with publication expectations will want both members of the couple to have published.

In some instances, shared positions appear to meet the needs of both dual-career couples and the institution, as suggested by the following comments made by a provost in our study: "The faculty we have who are sharing positions are an asset to the university. Oftentimes they come from very good schools and have good academic reputations that precede them here. Their choices are more limited because not all schools will allow them to job-share. But we have found that they are a good idea because each member rarely works half time—both are usually committed and take the job seriously."

The scientists in the McNeil and Sher study were quite positive about the advantages of split or shared positions. Although stressing that such accommodations function best when the partners are at about the same career stage and that they work for people with specific needs and goals, McNeil and Sher could find little wrong with shared and split positions as a solution to the needs of dual-career academic couples. A closer look at Wildwood College and its approach to dual-career academic couples will provide a better understanding of how split and shared positions work. After this discussion, we will expand on their benefits and disadvantages.

The Wildwood Experience

"Wildwood," like many small colleges, accommodates dual-career academic couples by allowing them to share a single position in a manner that is a hybrid of the split and shared positions defined by McNeil and Sher. (Refer to chapter 3 for fuller description of "Wildwood.") At Wildwood, as at most places that allow couples to share positions, the couples themselves initiate the request. Typically a couple will apply with a cover letter explaining that they wish to be considered together for a single position. Vitae for both members of the couple are included, and if the department is interested in both they are invited to campus for an interview. For Wildwood to agree to let a couple share a position, both members need to be qualified. The departmental faculty vote on whether to hire the couple as a pair or to hire another of the final candidates. If the couple represents the "best hire" from the candidate pool, they are offered the shared position.

Under Wildwood's arrangement, each partner receives one-half of a single salary, but both partners are able to apply in their own right for the college's professional development fund and for research support. In addition, both partners have full benefits. In determining tenure and promotion, each partner is treated separately; it is conceivable, although this has never happened at Wildwood, that one partner could receive tenure while the other would not. The number of couples who share positions at Wildwood has varied over time. Currently the college has approximately eight married couples on its faculty, four of them in shared positions. To put these numbers in perspective, Wildwood currently employs eighty-nine full-time faculty members.

Technically, under the shared position arrangement at Wildwood each partner receives half of a regular salary, but this is not always the case in practice. Usually one partner or both will have opportunities to teach extra courses or to fill some other institutional need, and they are paid above their regular half-time faculty salary for such services. Because of its small size, couples who share a contract generally teach in the same discipline. Back in the mid-1840s when Wildwood was founded, its first two professors were husband and wife. But the college's policy on spousal accommodation was implemented in the 1970s. The policy originated with a faculty couple's need: the wife of a professor also wanted to teach. The basic requirements of this policy are that both partners be qualified for a position, teach in the same discipline, and be willing to share a single job.

Faculty members in split positions at Wildwood are evaluated separately for tenure. Everyone agreed that the worst possible scenario had not come to pass—that one member of the couple succeeded and the other did not. As a music professor noted, "Wildwood is quite careful not to put people on the tenure-track unless they are quite confident that they'll continue. The problem [of one spouse's getting tenure and the other not] is more a problem in theory than in fact." At Wildwood if one half of the partnership does leave, the other spouse is able to take on the full position, assuming the remaining spouse has tenure. This happened for one woman who has shared a position with her husband since the 1970s. He got into administration and liked it so much that he applied for, and got, an administrative post at another institution. The woman took over the faculty position at Wildwood full time, and they now have a commuter marriage.

Perceived Strengths of the Policy at Wildwood

From an institutional standpoint, Wildwood's approach is thought to be very successful, by both faculty and the administration. First, this approach helps the college meet staffing needs, as suggested by the following comment: "For us, joint appointments are often preferable. Especially in small colleges where you are always working with fractions of people, the joint appointments give you greater flexibility. So from the college's standpoint this works well." To this a college administrator added: "Oftentimes individuals don't just split one job. There are usually additional classes to be taught or some other need to be filled, and we can pay a person in addition to their regular one-half pay to do that. This, too, is good for us because we don't have to search for someone from outside the college."

Second, this approach is believed to have led to greater faculty diversity, as indicated in this administrator's reflection: "For us accommodating spouses has really been beneficial. We get so much more diversified faculty. . . . Especially here given our small departments, hiring a couple gives us more diversity in terms of outlook, personality, and expertise." As one of the couples cited by McNeil and Sher explained, "Two individuals bring two different ways of thinking, two different backgrounds, two different approaches, multiple skills, and generally much greater richness of experience than would be possible with a single individual" (1998, 15). According to several respondents, shared positions at Wildwood are a means of achieving gender balance on the faculty.

Third, there is the perception among some faculty that Wildwood's approach reduces the total cost for faculty salaries. This is a benefit to the institution but, as discussed in the next section, a concern for the affected faculty. Put simply, some believe that when the college hires a dual-career couple it gets two faculty members for the price of one. This perception is reflected in the following faculty comment:

> There is no doubt about it that the institution wins. I don't want to sound cynical, and this college has been very good to us in a lot of ways. But the fact is the institution gets two bodies working for one salary. So I'm always a little surprised when I hear that an institution is wary [about accommodating spouses in this way]. From my perspective . . . institutions get two for the price of one, while at the same time you are helping the couple. . . . The workload is like a gas that fills up the room. If your teaching load is fairly light then advising becomes really heavy.

Although no one at Wildwood specifically mentioned benefits to research funding, split and shared positions in fields or universities in which grant funding is necessary increase the number of faculty applying for funding.

Dual-career couples who share positions at Wildwood see the college's approach as successfully meeting many of their needs as well. This is consistent with the views of the scientists in McNeil and Sher's study. McNeil and Sher cite many advantages and few disadvantages and say, "Many people in such positions rave about them, write articles about them, and spread the gospel about how wonderful shared/split positions are" (1998, 14). Why do couples like this arrangement so much? Above all, the couples at Wildwood are very happy to have jobs at a single institution rather than facing one partner's commuting to another institution, let alone the prospect of underemployment or unemployment. Unexpectedly, several professors remarked that a great benefit of Wildwood's approach is that both partners are regarded as equal and fully contributing members of the faculty. They contrasted this view with that at other institutions where one partner was regarded as the "real" or "leading" academic while the other was seen as merely an "accompanying spouse." The comment below, which was prompted by the question, "What do you like about Wildwood's policy?" is representative of this perceived benefit:

> Well, avoiding the rather rampant abuses of how this is often done elsewhere. . . . Other places where we've worked one of us has worked full time and the other has been brought on board to teach a course or two. That [part-time] person has been treated with considerable condescension by other faculty members. Here that's not the case. We're both just on the faculty. . . . We were at [X university] for a number of years and we'd go to some kind of social affair at which faculty and spouses were present. My wife was generally treated as someone not to have a serious conversation about [our discipline] with—even though her qualifications are every bit as strong as [those of] anyone there—simply because she was the so-called accompanying spouse. Here that's not the case. . . . We're treated, both of us, as human beings and academics.

In some instances, working closely with one's spouse was also viewed as a benefit of Wildwood's approach to accommodating dual-career couples. One professor who described working with her husband as a "joy" also pointed out that he and she could each teach the classes in their area that they enjoyed the most but could also count on the other to cover classes in case of illness or an emergency. In brief, sharing a single position was perceived as giving an academic couple more flexibility on the job. Some of the couples cited by McNeil and Sher expand on this theme of flexibility. Split and shared positions are particularly beneficial for those with young children. They allow both spouses to pursue legitimate scholarly careers in teaching, research, and service while leaving them more time to spend with their children.

Shared and split positions also are perceived as having much greater status, if less salary, than visiting, non-tenure-track positions. Typically, both partners participate in the full range of faculty activities and have voting rights. Although not mentioned by faculty commenting on shared appointments at Wildwood, an added advantage of these appointments identified by McNeil and Sher is that they allow both partners to pursue serious academic careers, including obtaining research funding. Except for worries about salary, the faculty who job-share at Wildwood did not express any feelings of marginalization, isolation, or special vulnerability; indeed, several remarked that they felt fully integrated into the faculty ranks. It is likely that the administration and "regular" faculty have contributed significantly to their half-time colleagues' sense of full inclusion at the institution. First, administrators and full-time faculty have made a conscious decision not to make any status distinctions based on whether someone is full time or half time. They also avoid making status distinctions about spouses who job-share. In fact, an administrator at the college even remarked that he found it distasteful to use terms such as "lead and trailing spouse" and "primary and secondary hire." At Wildwood, we did not hear one faculty member use these or similar expressions to set apart faculty in shared positions. In addition, job-sharing faculty are integrated into every facet of faculty life. These are not people who are expected to teach their classes and then quietly disappear; rather, they are regarded as, and act as, fully participating members of the campus community.

Given its relatively small size and somewhat isolated location, it is understandable that places like Wildwood would adopt a position-sharing approach to spouse and partner accommodation. The culture at Wildwood seems to be implicated in the relative success of this approach (as perceived by faculty and administration). This institution has a long tradition of decision making through consensus, so everyone has a genuine influence in personnel and policy decisions. Another characteristic of Wildwood's culture is that it is far less bureaucratic than most contemporary colleges and universities. In contrast to the situation at more bureaucratized institutions, the needs of personnel tend to be addressed as they arise, and there is room for more individualized responses. The same holds true for meeting certain institutional needs, particularly concerning staffing. Thus, within the basic framework of its accommodation policy, Wildwood maintains room for flexibility.

While there are cultural and other features of Wildwood that appear especially conducive to position sharing, other types of colleges and universities also have successfully used this approach to accommodation. As Katterman (1995) notes:

> [Many married couples] have been involved in sharing a single tenure-track position in the sciences. Most such arrangements, which also occasionally involve non-married pairs of scientists, generally occur at small liberal arts colleges, but some large research universities have also made room for this practice. The reports from the trenches are that shared or split positions are professionally and personally successful. The obvious hurdles of how to handle tenure decisions, how to assign fringe benefits, and how to live on one salary apparently are being solved to the satisfaction of both the faculty members and the institutions.

Perceived Weaknesses of Wildwood's Policy

Neither administrators nor faculty perceived that Wildwood's accommodation policy had any serious negative effects on the college as an institution. One administrator imagined that the most distressing possible outcome would be if one partner in the dual-career couple was successful and the other was not: "We've not had the experience that's everyone's worst nightmare; that is, where one person is much better than the other." Administrators at Wildwood are more concerned about the lack of opportunities for nonacademic, professional partners: "Our problem has been less with people who want to share appointments and more with lack of other local employment options. Where someone is an artist or a psychoanalyst, and so the couple lives in [a big city some seventy miles away] and commutes. Because of the residential character of the college that can be a problem."

Couples at Wildwood had two concerns about shared and split positions. The first was salary, and the second was workload. Most expressed a concern about salary or said that even though they were technically working only half time, in reality they were working as much or nearly as much as regular full-time faculty. As indicated in the following comments, however, these concerns were qualified, often with a positive assessment of Wildwood's willingness to accommodate dual-career couples and an acknowledgment that the couple did *choose* to share a contract. Regarding salary considerations, the following comment is typical:

> The greatest drawback to [sharing a position] is salary. Someday we'll have to put kids through college. Someday we'll have to retire. And we won't have the built-up savings that two-job couples have. . . . Now there are benefits that both spouses get and that cost [Wildwood] more than if two people were not sharing a position. For instance, we both get to have a conference allowance . . . and then there are small bits of research money and we are treated like separate people for that purpose.

In regard to the concern about working more than half time, the following comments are representative:

> I'm here as early as everybody else and I'm here as late as everybody else even though I'm teaching a reduced load. But this is our decision [to share a single position and to work as hard as we do]. No one is forcing us to be here. No one would confront us if we really did just work half time, but [as] the kind of people we are it's hard to say we're going to put half of ourselves into this job. And I do feel able to say "no" when it comes to committee assignments, and that's where we pull out the card that says, "Look I'm only half time, you're not going to dump on me a full committee assignment."

Another professor expressed similar feelings about working more than half time:

> I never felt like I was part time, even though technically I was teaching two courses less than a full-time person. . . . But we did get just one salary and split it. . . . This [is the] sort of "taking advantage of" which periodically one might feel is also somewhat self-imposed. For me, I was just consumed with my work here, my love for [Wildwood], and my love for teaching that I just never paid that much attention [to making one-half of a regular salary].

Concluding Comment

In sum, if handled properly, shared and split positions seem to offer more advantages than disadvantages for both institutions and faculty couples. Despite economic disadvantages to the couple and the need to be aware of the potential expectation that a half-time faculty member will do a full-time job for half pay, split and shared positions seem to offer an excellent solution for certain couples and institutions. They probably would not work for everyone or for every institution, and it would probably not be desirable for a college to have too many faculty in these types of appointments. However, shared and split appointments seem to offer some real benefits in the right circumstances.

The relative benefits to faculty of shared and split appointments depend largely on the needs and preferences of the faculty themselves. These appointments will be especially attractive to couples who feel comfortable living on less than two full salaries and who place considerable value on activities outside their paid employment. Perhaps more than any other alternative, shared and split appointments enable individuals to achieve a balance between their work and home lives. Such positions are also not likely to be stigmatizing because neither member of the couple is considered the initial or the accompanying spouse. Rather, the two are hired simultaneously. From an institutional standpoint, there are also benefits to allowing couples to share a single position. Shared positions are economical in that institutions can hire two people for nearly the price of one. They also help provide greater diversity of experience and perspectives within the faculty, which can be more difficult to achieve at smaller institutions than at larger places.

7 | Accommodation through Shared Advertising

Craig and Mary were both completing their dissertations in Japanese literature and were thinking seriously about academic employment opportunities. They were reasonably hopeful that they would both be hired into tenure-track positions. After all, they were graduating from a top program, had already published several articles, and had influential advisers. Yet Craig and Mary knew that their chances of both being hired at the same institution were remote. How many schools advertised for a single position in Japanese, let alone two?

Although they did not have children, the couple had decided that in no circumstances would they accept jobs requiring them to live apart. One alternative might be to share a single position, but having supported themselves throughout the graduate school years, and feeling the financial burden of five years' worth of student loans, a shared appointment—and a single income—seemed unworkable. Adjunct or short-term appointments were unattractive for the same reason; the couple needed two real incomes that they could count on for the long run. Perusing a journal, Craig noticed that four northeastern colleges shared an advertisement listing fifteen positions in various disciplines. Included on the list were two positions in Japanese. The ad mentioned that all four institutions were within an easy commute of an hour and a half. Although the advertised positions were at different colleges, the drive sounded doable, and it was certainly preferable to the alternatives they had imagined.

Craig and Mary applied for both jobs. To their astonishment, they both were granted interviews at the two schools. Throughout the interview process, neither mentioned having a spouse who was also seeking an academic position in Japanese. Within the month, Craig and Mary were each offered a contract, and both accepted. Although they would be working at different schools, they were happy to have found two regular tenure-track positions within easy commuting distance.

An option for colleges with limited resources for hiring both members of a dual-career couple is the joint advertising of academic positions among colleges in the same geographic region. This sharing of information and advertising resources is usually done by colleges that are close to one another. The Claremont Colleges, for example, a formal consortium of five undergraduate institutions and a freestanding graduate school (Claremont McKenna College, Pomona College, Scripps College, Pitzer College, Harvey Mudd College, and the Claremont Graduate University), post a large advertisement in the Chronicle of Higher Education every fall in which all the colleges list tenure-track openings. Their particular advertisement does not explicitly mention dual-career couples, but its stated purpose, according to their representatives, is to make it clear to an academic couple considering the area that, if there was a match between one partner's needs and the college's needs, the other would have some employment options nearby. Other institutions we know of that use this approach include the Ohio 5 (Denison, Ohio Wesleyan, Kenyon, College of Wooster, and Oberlin), the five-college consortium in Massachusetts (University of Massachusetts, Amherst, Smith, Mount Holyoke, and Hampshire), and a trio of colleges in Maine (Bates, Colby, and Bowdoin). Some of the advertisements placed by these consortia are explicit about attracting dual-career couples. They start with a tag line reading, "Attention Dual-Career Academic Couples." For example, Bates College, Bowdoin College, and Colby College, all within commuting distance of one another, advertise jointly. Their ad in a recent Chronicle of Higher Education reads: "Bates, Bowdoin, and Colby Colleges are conducting searches for faculty appointments beginning fall 2002. The following information may be particularly useful for dual-career academic couples. All three schools are located within one hour of each other, and within a two to three hour commute of Boston." Staff members at the Chronicle of Higher Education classifieds division reported an increase in such advertisements over the past several years, showing that this practice is growing in popularity.

Assessing the effectiveness of such advertisements is difficult because any one academic dean would not necessarily know if a spouse or partner of a recruited faculty member had found employment at another college. This is in large part because hiring is conducted separately at each college within such consortia, without the explicit input of those outside. Unlike attempting to find a tenure-track position within the same institution, where one dean or a provost can exert some pressure on a fellow dean or department chair to at least consider hiring an accompanying spouse or partner, institutions in a consortium have no such agreement or ability to exhort their neighbors. Furthermore, search committees don't know whether these consortium advertisements or some other means of advertising a faculty position have led a candidate to apply. Nor will they necessarily know that the candidate has a spouse or partner applying for a position at another member of the consortium.

Nevertheless, deans believe these advertisements are a good investment for several reasons. First, they signal to couples that there are other employment opportunities nearby. This, they believe, helps to make these institutions more attractive to a broader pool of candidates. This is especially so when institutions are in somewhat isolated locations. Second, the ads indicate, many of them explicitly, concern about dual-career couples. Signaling to potentially strong hires that these institutions care about their needs might also help attract good candidates. Third, the act of creating such advertisements enhances communication among the different institutions, which the deans see as a way of addressing the limited opportunities available at any one particular college.

To learn more about joint advertising and consortia, we spoke with deans at several colleges that engage in joint advertising. Those we spoke with reported a relatively high level of cooperation—at least in sharing vitae for potential hires and discussing such hires. At the same time, they also reported that any particular college would be unwilling to circumvent a regular hiring process to help out another college and would not want to ask search committees to look more favorably on a candidate whose partner was being recruited by another local college. That said, there was some sense of cooperation between institutions, which was seen as good public relations. Cost savings is another benefit of joint advertising of academic positions. According to the advertising director at the *Chronicle of Higher Education*, placing a shared ad rather than a number of separate ones would save some money.

Accommodating academic spouses by making them aware of faculty positions at nearby institutions requires, of course, that there be such institutions. But this approach to spouse and partner accommodation takes practically no effort other than placing advertisements in the appropriate outlets. One of the main advantages of cooperating in this way is that institutions are more likely to retain faculty; couples who find a workable solution to their situation are more likely to stay put. And there are many benefits for couples who can take advantage of the consortium approach. Each partner receives a full salary and benefits, along with the full range of research support, equipment, and so on that normally accompanies a faculty position. These faculty also avoid all the negatives associated with adjunct and short-term appointments, as well as any suspicion from the "regular hires." These faculty *are* regular hires.

Concluding Comment

The consortium approach avoids the problems associated with hiring faculty spouses in adjunct and temporary positions. For the institution, all it entails is placing advertisements that alert prospective applicants to the positions available within a reasonable commute. Their application and hiring processes need not be changed. Faculty who are hired thereby avoid any stigma they might encounter with more intervention. These appointments will be especially attractive to individuals who desire regular tenure-track placement close to their faculty spouses or partners. Of course couples will have to rely on a little luck to land tenure-track positions from two institutions at the same time. When it works, however, appointments resulting from joint advertising are no different from conventional appointments.

8 | In Pursuit of Tenure-Track Positions

Natalie and Aaron, like many academic couples, met and later married while attending the same graduate school. Natalie was getting her doctorate in English and Aaron was getting his in history. Both were ambitious and determined to find tenure-track positions in their fields at research universities. Yet given that the academic labor market in both English and history was still tight, they were worried about ending up apart, having to commute long distances and seeing each other only on weekends, or having one of them settle for a position that was less than ideal.

Natalie and Aaron's worry intensified when the two began to apply for positions in their respective fields. As Natalie's adviser declared one day, "It doesn't take a Ph.D. to realize that if there are 250 applicants for every job, the chances of you and your spouse being selected out of the 500 applicants are astronomical." Rejection letter after rejection letter arrived, and their frustration grew.

After many long and worrisome months, Natalie interviewed for a position at Riverdale University. She felt pretty confident about how the interview had gone and thought there was a good chance she would be offered the job. She was further heartened because the institution was "dual-career couple friendly." The initial position posting had included a statement about the institution's willingness to try to help academic couples. Then, during the interview process, the department chair mentioned the institution's dual-career policy.

During their final meeting, Natalie told the chair that her spouse had received his doctorate in history and was now also looking for a tenure-track position. The department chair offered to look at Aaron's vita and to start exploring any job openings at the institution. Natalie saw this as a good sign and went home to await further news—both about her situation and about a potential position for Aaron.

Natalie was subsequently offered the job. And the department chair, as promised, had sent Aaron's vita to the History Department chair. The History Department chair was favorably impressed by Aaron's vita but was not ready to recommend that the department forgo an open search and make a direct hire.

Instead, she offered Aaron an adjunct position with a term appointment. Feeling that this was the best option available, Natalie and Aaron accepted the jobs.

Two years have passed, and Natalie is happily ensconced in her tenure-track position. Aaron has continued to publish in his field despite a heavy teaching load and frustration over not yet being on tenure track. On a positive note, the History Department posted a tenure-track position that Aaron applied for, and he is being seriously considered. Aaron and Natalie are optimistic that luck will come their way and that both will be fully employed within the next year. If Aaron gets the job they plan to stay at the institution, realizing that lightning won't strike twice.

The holy grail of dual-career accommodations, especially when both members want academic appointments, is two tenure-track positions at the same institution. To say that such a find is elusive, especially when both partners are new to the profession and have yet to be seen as academic stars, seems an understatement. A tight academic labor market in many fields, with too many qualified applicants for too few tenure-track positions, makes finding two jobs together seem difficult if not impossible. Nonetheless, our survey of chief academic officers did yield a few examples of institutions that hired dual-career academic couples into two full-time tenure-track positions. This happened in three ways: through happenstance, through an ad hoc intervention by an administrator, or through a formal policy providing for such accommodations.

In most cases, both faculty members were described as having "gotten lucky" and having received tenure-track positions at the same institution with no intervention. Either there were two tenure-track positions available at the same time, or one partner took a tenure-track job and the other found a position later. More often than not, luck took a while to take effect. In fact the accompanying spouse was often described as being in a holding pattern—for example, working as an adjunct or in a part-time position until a suitable tenure-track opening became available. In our survey of AAC&U institutions, one provost at a research university described a case where the spouse of an already employed faculty member applied for and was hired in the college of physical and mathematical sciences. In this case the spouse had worked in adjunct and temporary positions for a few years until her department posted a position for which she was qualified. After a national search and a review of the qualifications of the applicants, the department decided that she was the most qualified and granted her the job. In a similar example, a chief academic officer of a comprehensive institution hired a faculty member in a tenure-track position and offered the spouse a non-tenure-track position as a lecturer. The provost explained further: "Now a position has opened, and the spouse has moved to a tenure-track position." Similarly, another provost offered this example: "A couple of years ago a potential faculty member in business had a 'trailing spouse' who was given a non-tenure-track position. The next year she chose to go through a search for a tenure-track position rather than exercise the spousal option, even though the college was willing to appoint her. She felt she would be stigmatized without the search." She got the job. Most of the provosts who wrote about having hired academic couples were at institutions without formal policies or even regular practices.

Policies for Creating Tenure-Track Positions for Accompanying Spouses and Partners

Several larger research universities have recently developed policies and procedures to create and fund tenure-track positions for qualified accompanying spouses or partners. In our survey, sixteen institutions reported having policies that allow for creating a tenure-track position for some "highly qualified" academic couples. The definition of highly qualified varies slightly from institution to institution, but it is clear from the survey results that such accommodations are most likely to be made to recruit those who are more senior—academic stars—rather than those newer to the field. Some institutions, however, did describe creating tenure-track positions for the partners of highly sought-after junior faculty as well. At one institution with such a policy, a chair of the English Department offered an assistant professorship to a person whose spouse had just completed a degree in history. The dean of the College of Liberal Arts proposed giving a new faculty line to the History Department, offering to pay one-third of the expense from college funds if the History Department and the English Department together paid the rest from their budgets. The hire was made. Two other institutions in our survey reported similar cost sharing for hiring an accompanying spouse or partner between the provost, the initial hire's department, and the partner's department. As one explained, "When we make an accommodation that involves funding a position, we try to use a cost-sharing approach. Ideally [sharing is based on] a one-third hiring unit, one-third faculty member's unit, one-third provost split. Fairly frequently the allocation will change . . . with a decreasing amount paid by the provost." The assumption here is that the central administration is subsidizing the position until the department hiring the accompanying spouse or partner can assume the cost of the line. One might compare the provost's share to a low-interest loan to the department to cover the up-front costs of an unplanned position.

In addition to the institutions identified through our survey as having formal policies for creating and funding tenure-track positions for accompanying spouses and partners, an Internet search yielded several other research universities with formalized dual-career accommodation policies that allow departments to create tenure-track positions. These include the University of Arizona, Pennsylvania State University, Washington State University, the University of Wisconsin, the University of Michigan, and the University of Illinois, to name a few. The amount of information on the Internet about each of these policies varies considerably, but some common patterns seem to hold. These include making the candidate aware that such a policy exists, obtaining information about the qualifications and interests of the spouse or partner, allowing the faculty in the target department to review the qualifications and decide if they wish to hire the accompanying spouse or partner, and some sort of cost sharing to pay for the position.

Differences among Dual-Career Tenure-Track Hiring Policies

A few variations in these policies are worth noting. First, some institutions explicitly mention the policy to all candidates in order to avoid making applicants disclose their marital or partner status. At other institutions with such policies, it is left to the candidate to mention the employment needs of a spouse or partner. A further twist is offered by the University of California, Davis (UCD), which has created an office to shepherd the creation of new positions for dual-career couples through institutional channels (to the potential department head of the accompanying partner, to the relevant deans, through the equal opportunity office, to the chief academic officer, etc.). In contrast to most policies, which place the burden on the department chair of the initial hire, officials at UCD seem to have decided that having a centralized office might lead to fewer political difficulties and make the procedure more uniform across hiring units. Further, administrators at UCD suggest that a centralized office eases accommodations across schools and departments as well as within academic units.

The University of Illinois at Urbana-Champaign is among the research universities that have created a formal procedure and a funding mechanism to hire dual-career academic couples in tenure-track positions (Loeb 1997). A study of its policy is the only published research on the outcomes associated with a dual-career hiring program that emphasizes the creation of tenure-track positions. The University of Illinois policy was created by administrators who recognized that in order to recruit the best faculty, the institution needed to be proactive in meeting the needs of dual-career couples. This was deemed especially important given the university's relatively isolated location (Loeb 1997). In an evaluation of the outcomes associated with this program, Loeb explains that the institution's practice of hiring dual-career academic couples began in the early 1980s as an ad hoc approach to recruiting desirable faculty members. Though negotiated case by case, the funding for new positions typically entailed having the central administration provide bridge funding of up to one-third of a position, while the other departments involved would ante up the remaining two-thirds. The assumption underlying this arrangement was that the department hiring the accompanying spouse would eventually (usually within three years) cover the faculty member's salary through its own budget line, often when a senior faculty member retired. This practice became more routinized in the early 1990s. According to Loeb's evaluation (the results are presented in chapter 1), the University of Illinois approach to hiring dual-career couples is a success in that it has helped the institution recruit and retain faculty it otherwise might have lost.

We report here two cases of institutions that take different approaches to creating tenure-track positions for spouses and partners: Riverdale University and Hilltop University. The policies share some similarities, but they are different enough that a thorough description of each seems useful and informative.

Tenure-Track Faculty Accommodations at Riverdale University

"Riverdale," a land-grant research university, is one of the handful of institutions in the country that offers a formal program to assist in the hiring of an accompanying spouse into a tenure-track position. (See chapter 3 for fuller description of "Riverdale University.") The Bridge Program, as it is called, provides a mechanism for accommodating qualified spouses seeking tenure-track faculty appointments. Although in practice Riverdale may accommodate unmarried couples—either heterosexual or gay and lesbian—the policy explicitly uses the word "spouse." As the associate provost explained, "——— is a very conservative state. We use the word spouse." The purpose of the Bridge Program, established in 1992, is "to help academic departments recruit and retain dual-career couples when both spouses seek faculty positions." The program accomplishes this by providing financial assistance for three years to a department willing to hire the accompanying spouse. After the three years, the department must pick up the entire cost of the faculty line.

Little is written about the Bridge Program, and its existence is not widely publicized, but several administrators were familiar enough with it to explain how it works. According to the associate provost, the program originated because "there were a number of people that we wanted to attract to our faculty that had spouses, and their spouses' employment was as important to them as their own employment. So we figured this is a piece of it and we need to make some things happen." One dean said he would be as likely to invoke the Bridge Program for a junior faculty member as for a senior one, although there was some disagreement among deans on this point. Others suggested that the difficult process would more likely be invoked to attract a "known quantity [read more senior faculty member] than to recruit a newly minted Ph.D."

The first step to enacting the policy at Riverdale is identifying the need to accommodate a spouse in a faculty position. At Riverdale it is the responsibility of the potential hire to initiate this discussion. The Bridge Program is not mentioned unless a candidate asks for help in finding academic work for a spouse. Once the hiring committee or department chair becomes aware of this situation, "Normally, you call the appropriate place [department] because as you are aware, with a faculty hire it is not something that is dictated. The best you can do is make the information available and hope that on the other end they will be receptive and give it a good look." According to this dean, people at Riverdale try hard to be receptive. "It doesn't mean that the faculty will make any exceptions in terms of quality, but they will certainly at least have a look at the résumé . . . and if it looks like a reasonably good hire they will go ahead with it." This dean indicated that if someone contacted him about a spousal accommodation he would send the résumé to the appropriate department, which would evaluate the résumé. If the department expected a retirement in the next couple of years or could foresee the person's meeting a programmatic need, then an interview would be arranged.

The schools involved and the provost work out the financial arrangements. Typically, each party contributes one-third of the accompanying spouse's salary for up to three years. That is, the initial hire's unit contributes one-third, the unit hiring the accompanying spouse pays one-third, and the provost throws in the remaining one-third. The associate provost noted that these percentages could vary depending on the financial situation of any one of the players. "If the trailing spouse was in English, we would transfer each year one-third of the salary to English unless the English Department had more funds available now, in which case we might chip in less. The understanding is that the unit employing the accompanying spouse anticipates having a tenure-track position within the three-year time period that this individual will fill."

When it is likely that departments or schools will make a deal, the Provost's Office becomes involved. Departments have to demonstrate that they will have an opening in the near future because, as the associate provost explained,

> the Bridge Program only works in terms of the permanent appointment. . . . There is a three-way discussion [among the provost and the two units involved]. . . . If engineering really wants the engineering candidate they put in some money on a non-recurring basis. Again, they are going to have to help because the English Department hadn't planned on having this opportunity thrust upon them. Everybody needs to buy in on it. And this is the piece the provost handles himself. He is the person most familiar with all of the school budgets, and he knows what sort of funds they have. . . . This program came out of our office, and the notion is to try and make things happen, not to be a roadblock with it.

Riverdale is careful not to do anything to make accompanying spouses seem special in any way or as if they are in positions created specially for them. Every attempt is made to fully involve all departmental faculty in the decision making. As the associate provost noted, "The Bridge Program is a financial arrangement, and it is a very invisible financial arrangement so the person who comes in on it doesn't have the feeling that they are part of a bridge program."

The provost and the Office of Affirmative Action work closely together on bridge hires. Because of Riverdale's low percentage of women and minority faculty, it is usually possible to approve a waiver for an official search in bridge cases. A memorandum from the Chancellor's Office to all vice chancellors, deans, directors, and department heads at Riverdale specifies the need to obtain a special waiver from the Office of Affirmative Action in order to create a temporary or permanent faculty position, delay or forgo a search for an existing vacancy, or insert a candidate into an existing search as a means to recruit or retain sought-after faculty. The request for such a waiver has to be preapproved by the relevant department chairs and deans and by the chancellor before being approved by the Office of Affirmative Action. In addition, the memo specifies that the person has to be qualified for the position and that hiring the couple must support the institution's commitment to affirmative action and excellence. The program works because no one is asked to compromise on quality. As the acting vice president of human relations said, "The important thing is to build into the system a mechanism so that the faculty considering the trailing spouse has full input into the decision so if the trailing spouse is hired, he or she does indeed become a full-fledged colleague. . . . They have to feel like this is something they will really want." And, "Eventually they [department or school] are going to have to pay for the line."

While the exact number of those assisted is unknown, we were told that some units use the Bridge Program frequently. One dean told us that he had four or five faculty currently benefiting from the arrangement. At the same time, others seemed unaware of its existence. The associate provost did tell us that the provost sets aside a pool of bridge money and that so far that pool has not been exhausted. Riverdale has kept no data on the number of accommodations requested or granted or on who takes advantage of the policy. They could not say how often an initial hire was male or female, of beginning rank or of more senior stature. Nor were they aware of trends in which departments or schools sought accommodations or how successful accommodation attempts have been. According to a member of the central administration, the institution purposely did not collect these data because they did not want to stigmatize those who have benefited from the program. As such, the administration at Riverdale has opted just to assume that the policy works. For an outside observer, this makes it hard to evaluate the program from a retention or recruitment perspective.

Perceived Strengths of the Bridge Program at Riverdale

During our site visit we heard very few complaints or concerns about the policy itself. It is widely believed that the Bridge Program is a tool to help the institution recruit and retain good faculty. According to a dean, "We view it as a competitive advantage if we can, in fact, offer a dual-career couple assistance. . . . We are in fact looking for the best people in the country, and they have no problems finding jobs even before the economy got so hot. And so we are always in competition with a number of places." This administrator also credits the program for helping with retention. "The other thing is if you successfully do this, our retention rate will be higher because [finding two tenure-track jobs] is difficult to do. . . . Even though someone may be reluctant to mention that they have a trailing spouse, from my point of view, it is fine. We really like them to tell us."

The other benefit of the Bridge Program is that it forces academic units to think about their faculty needs in advance and engage in some strategic planning. Indeed, for departments to take advantage of the Bridge Program they must satisfactorily demonstrate to the central administration that, owing to retirements or student demand, they are likely to have a future need for a faculty member with the same specialization as the accompanying spouse or partner. This is essential because the Bridge Program offers money only to temporarily fund the position.

Perceived Weaknesses of Riverdale's Policy

One of the questions respondents raised was what the institution would do if one member of a dual-career couple received tenure and the other did not. However, no one said that this problem had occurred. There was also some concern that the program is not aggressively marketed—that not everyone knows about it. Indeed, respondents were at least somewhat worried by the lack of communication about the policy. It is our understanding that the specifics of the program are kept quiet and vague in order to minimize the stigma of being accommodated, to allow maximum flexibility in how to accommodate, and to limit the requests for assistance to those cases that truly warrant such accommodations. The Bridge Program was described several times as not being open to everyone—as reserved for recruiting the "best" initial hire and only the most qualified spouses to join the Riverdale faculty. The potential inequitable use of the policy by departments with more clout than others may exacerbate existing class differences among faculty. Another weakness inherent in the policy is that it takes a rather long time to make all the arrangements necessary to hire the accompanying spouse. Although no one said this had happened, one could imagine that the institution might lose a good candidate while a position for his or her spouse was being approved.

Hilltop University's Dual-Career Hiring Policy

"Hilltop University," a flagship research university, began its existing, unwritten dual-career policy in 1993 under the influence of its president. (See chapter 3 for a fuller description of "Hilltop University.") Before this policy was established, Hilltop had hired dual-career academics using ad hoc measures. The president had started a similar program during his presidency at another research university; but at least one of the deans also claims some credit for it: "[He] had just become president in January.... He appoints me in March . . . I officially take over in September. . . . I knew about the program at X University, so when the department chair called me and said we may have difficulty getting [the principal hire] because we are having difficulty finding a job for her husband, I didn't know the provost but I called [the president] and said, 'You know the program we had at X, why can't we do something like that here,' and he said, 'Why, I don't know why we can't.'"

According to records kept by the Provost's Office at Hilltop, sixteen faculty couples had been accommodated under the current dual-career policy when we collected our data. This figure probably underestimates the number of academic couples on campus because it fails to account for hires that were made without the assistance of the central administration and it does not include academics whose spouses are employed in non-tenure-track lines. However, given the size of the university and the perceived need for such a policy, that very few couples actually participate suggests that Hilltop uses its policy judiciously and selectively.

The policy, though unwritten, is enacted quite uniformly. In its most basic sense, it operates in the following manner: "The college recruiting the lead member of the spousal team would put up a third of the trailing spouse's salary. The receiving department or college would put up a third, and the provost would put up a third." Unlike Riverdale, where the policy operates as a bridge program, here sharing of the funding to create a new position involves the permanent transfer of funds from one college to another. As one department chair noted, "It comes out of our budget every year. . . . A chunk of our instructional budget was excised." The provost's money comes from "an unallocated teaching salary pool that we hold back every year, and the size of it varies." This fund is also used for things like counteroffers.

In terms of enacting the policy, most respondents agreed that considering a dual-career hire begins at the department level. As one dean explained, "When my department says to me [that] we want to hire somebody and it gets serious, usually before the interview or at the interview, we find out if there is a spouse. I ask the chair to call the other department to see if they will interview that spouse, and I immediately call the dean. And what happens is that there has to be agreement all around. That means that the department of the second person has to want that person." Similarly, a department chair explained: "If a department wanted to hire someone who had a spouse who is also interested in an academic job, the chair would contact the chair of the department that would be appropriate for that spouse and ask if they had an interest in looking at the vita. They could say yes or no. If they say yes, then there would be some conversation at the dean's level in the respective colleges to which those departments belonged. And if everyone seems agreeable there would be an approach to the provost."

Getting departments to agree to hire a spouse is no simple matter. First, the department making the initial hire has to decide that it wants the person so much that it would be willing to ask another department to consider hiring the spouse. The department that wants the initial hire also has to be willing to give up one-third of the salary of the trailing spouse. This is typically decided through a vote by the department of the initial hire. The complexity of such a decision is highlighted by a case in which a department wanted to hire a promising assistant professor whose spouse was a more senior, better-known faculty member. As the chair explained, "That [the accompanying spouse] was a pretty serious guy who was getting paid some pretty serious money—he was getting paid, at that time, probably twenty thousand more than anyone on our faculty. This was in a different department that paid much better." The dean went on to explain that the one-third that his department contributed to the salary of the spouse was "enough that it was a junior line."

Once the initial department expresses an interest in making a hire, then the department hiring the spouse has to determine if it really wants the person in a tenure-track faculty line. Typically, the spouse will be invited to campus, will go through a compete interview, and will give a "job talk," a presentation in which the applicant discusses his or her research and approaches to teaching. Then the hiring department must vote—just as they would with any new hire. As an associate dean explained: "Although the person has an entrée into the process . . . they go through the same validation in our school as they would if they had gone through the longer entrée into the process. . . . Rather than [the department] getting a letter [from the candidate] saying 'I would like to apply for job' there is an immediate introduction. But beyond that there is no explicit accommodation. There were not changes in our standards." In other words, the accompanying spouse or partner is introduced as a potential candidate for a faculty position by the dean or department chair of the initial hire rather than applying for a position from the outside. Despite this "immediate introduction," the selection process remains as it would be in any regular search. That the department must want to hire the spouse was reiterated in almost every interview. As an administrator explained: "It really is a question of both departments feeling comfortable. . . . You can never force someone on a department, and as a dean I would not do that. . . . The point of this is not to make people unhappy. It is to make people happy." Similarly, a faculty member stated that when looking at a spousal hiring candidate, "I think people have a sense of the person's achievements and at least we do want to look at them on an absolute scale and try not to compromise. That is where there will be problems if a department feels like it is compromising academically, and in those cases I think they would vote against it no matter what, even though [they are only paying for] a third of a position."

All respondents at Hilltop stressed the importance of making sure that the spouse was of sufficient quality to warrant a tenure-track position. Typically the department asked to hire the accompanying spouse uses criteria comparable to those used in any hiring decision. According to someone in central administration: "In our Sociology Department, which is a good department, they just sort of declare that if the person would not make a short list, we're not going—it's not worth the bargain of getting a full-time person for one-third the salary." Most respondents stressed the importance of maintaining the standards of the department. As a faculty member explained, "You can't be doing it [hiring the person] just to satisfy the other department because the [hire] is going to be with you forever."

It is important to note that the policy at Hilltop is not written, which was described as "in keeping with the culture of the institution." Nonetheless, most respondents agreed that the university had regularized the practice in such a way as to make it well known at least among the deans. According to one dean, "If you asked a rank-and-file faculty member, they probably won't know at all. If you ask a dean, he or she probably knows about it." Several respondents suggested that it is likely that department chairs are unaware of the policy—they are made aware only if a dual-career situation arises in a search. According to one administrator: "We certainly have a practice . . . that we follow, and if a spousal hire situation comes up we try to accommodate as best we can." Similarly, a department chair explained that while the policy is not in writing, it is much more formal than it was in the past. He explained: "It is better to have a procedure if you are talking about building an institution over the long term. Ah, and the rule also, the practice gives something that department chairs can invoke. They know they can go to the President's Office . . . and they know they can go to the college."

While there is a typical procedure for securing a position at Hilltop, it is occasionally circumvented. For example, sometimes the Provost's Office refuses to put up its share of the funds, even when two departments are in agreement about making a dual-career accommodation. As someone in central administration explained, "We handle this on a case-by-case basis, so if we have criteria we say it depends on the specifics." Part of it depends on the "perception on the part of the provost of whether the trailing college—or either college—how much money they have." As noted by the respondents, the formal dual-career policy is designed to assist dual-career hires across colleges—the decision by a particular department or departments within a school to make a dual-career hire is feasible but would not typically involve money from the Provost's Office. As an assistant dean of a college stated, "If it involves two departments within liberal arts, which is also a very likely occurrence, we don't approach the provost about that. We have to handle that ourselves. . . . It becomes fifty/fifty, which is also a little weird. What some of our departments want us to do is to keep it one-third/one-third/one-third, but let the administrative one-third come from the dean. . . . So it just gets talked about and we figure out what we think we can do." As a dean noted, "Any two departments can negotiate between them any solution they want where any department pays any department however much they want. Even if it doesn't involve the administration it can work."

Another instance when the policy is not necessarily invoked is "preemptive counteroffers." As an administrator explained, "The overall program's intention is for recruitment and not for people that are already here." That said, several of the dual-career hires that used the one-third cost sharing were made to keep faculty members at Hilltop. And though the policy is designed for spouses, most respondents noted that while the term "spouse" is used purposefully, there was no reason to believe that the one-third split would not also be used to accommodate domestic partners if they met all the quality criteria. Thus far there have been no accommodations made for unmarried couples, either heterosexual or same-sex.

In terms of who gets accommodated at Hilltop, most respondents agreed that because of the complicated and political nature of the policy, the initial hiring department must really want to recruit the initial hire. As such, many respondents said that the policy was more likely to be used to recruit a "star" than an assistant professor. As one professor explained: "I think, though, there is a general impetus to do a lot more to recruit senior faculty. I mean, recruiting a full professor or a chaired professor is a much bigger deal and you have more clout with the administration. If you do have the green light on such a recruitment, you would make extra efforts to make sure that it works. But the rule being there makes it possible at the junior level." An administrator added:

> When you have a more junior person, whether that is at the assistant or associate level, there's usually not the compelling reason to do that. There are other good people you can get at those lower levels. Again, it is a matter of limited resources. If we had unlimited resources, sure there is the best person we want for an assistant professor level, and she has a spouse or partner that she wants to bring here and we want her, so we'll get her. But there is not unlimited money. . . . There just isn't the extra money to go out and be extra accommodating for people unless there is some compelling reason to do that, and the compelling reason has been for a senior person.

Perceived Strengths of Hilltop's Policy

Generally speaking, both faculty and administrators involved with the policy at Hilltop were positive about the institution's approach to dual-career hiring. The deans, department chairs, and accommodated couples we spoke with agreed that having a policy was essential in the institution's efforts to compete with the coastal universities it perceives to be its peers. One person noted that even Nobel laureates have spouses who hold faculty positions, and that Hilltop's chances of recruiting such a person were enhanced if jobs were available for spouses. From an institutional perspective, respondents believed that the policy was effective in meeting its goal: the recruitment and retention of quality faculty members. The general sentiment was that "[because of the policy] we have been able to recruit some people we would not otherwise have." As an administrator explained, "It is a way of keeping [Hilltop] competitive with places that either have a program or don't. In one way or another it gives us greater flexibility in terms of trying to recruit the people we really want to recruit." It was also said to be a retention tool. Specifically, one respondent commented that "from a retention standpoint it is extremely successful because places that I might consider that would be a step up for

me don't necessarily have very good policies for hiring women or spouses."
An administrator added, "Once you get a spousal team it is easier to keep
them because it is so hard to move."

Another institutional benefit that respondents noted was improved communication between departments and colleges. As one faculty member explained, "Probably there are some benefits to the university of having people
in different schools actually talk to one another." Further, respondents commented that the institution benefits because the second hire is often of "star
quality" as well. One department chair explained, "I do not think of the second person as being lesser. I think of it, as when we hire both of them, we
want both of them. And it may be that the first person came to the attention
of one department faster than the other person did." Indeed, the department
hiring the spouse typically gets an exceptional faculty member at one-third
the cost. According to a faculty member, "They got a guy who is an astounding scholar—especially turned out to be even more so since he got here—an
astounding scholar and they hired him at one-third his salary. My chair was
just jumping around so proud of himself."

From the viewpoint of the faculty who have been accommodated, the policy is also positive. One faculty couple explained: "Well all I can say [is] I have
very strong loyalty to the institution and I think that was in place long before
we had the opportunity. And this is just one, at least from my personal perspective, this is just one of the many ways the university has supported me
throughout the years."

Perceived Weaknesses of Hilltop's Policy

While the policy met the institutional goals, respondents also highlighted
some weaknesses. One concern had to do with lingering hostility that might
be felt by faculty in the department that hires the accompanying spouse. A
dean stated, "I think the person had an additional barrier when they came in
because they weren't there under normal circumstances. They hadn't come
up through a full search, and so I suspect that some of their new colleagues
would look askance at them." Similarly, a department chair explained, "I am
not going to pretend that there aren't some faculty, even going through the
process, that afterwards won't say, 'Well, he or she was only hired because.
. . .' Not by everyone but there are those attitudes. I am not going to say there
aren't." The safeguard for this negative experience, according to respondents, is to make sure that the accompanying spouse possesses the credentials necessary to be successful in the department. A department chair ex-

plained: "In the cases of spousal hiring you have to look carefully at the credentials of the spouse, because in [some] cases, if the department that the spouse would work in is very negative or skeptical it could be a very hostile environment and that spouse may not get tenure and it could be very painful. It is not doing a favor to the couple if you give a position to someone who is not going to prove himself or herself to be good enough academically."

Given the scrutiny experienced by accompanying spouses, those who were accommodated believed that faculty concerns eventually quieted down as they proved themselves to be able scholars and good colleagues. Nonetheless, accommodated spouses did occasionally feel uncomfortable with how they achieved their position. As one explained: "It would be nice to get away from the stigma of being the 'trailing spouse.' It is something that hangs over my head, and I don't know if that will ever change. Not so much in my program area any more, although it did hang on for several years. However, the fact that I know we were hired here because of [my spouse] when I am a good scholar in my own right. . . . I will have to get over it."

One concern expressed by a minority of faculty respondents was that once a couple is accommodated they may feel trapped and unable to move to another institution. Several of the faculty couples said they were less likely to get good raises because administrators knew they were not mobile. As one professor explained:

> The only way I'm ever going to get up to the market salary I could get if I were single, independent is if I get another outside offer. . . . But I am in a double bind because I might be able to get an offer as if I were single by going on an interview somewhere but I would basically have to hide my wife's employment and even then if I get an offer it isn't clear that they would raise me to meet the outside offer because they know I wouldn't leave unless we both got offers and that is extremely hard to do. . . . So I don't have a viable threat and I won't get a viable raise.

Last, while many noted that the policy's being unwritten was consistent with the culture of Hilltop, others said they would prefer to have it in writing. The political nature of who gets accommodated and who does not and who finds out about the policy and who does not was of particular concern to some faculty members. As one noted: "If you are going to talk about weaknesses, it is possible with this kind of flexible policy to play favorites—favoritism of some kind because it matters who you know and how persuasive your particular chair or dean is or not." While we did not interview dual-career faculty who were not accommodated, one can assume that they might feel some resentment at not being accorded the same accommodation given to stars. As we discuss in chapter 9, having an unwritten policy brings up concerns about fairness and about the potential for abuses and inequities among departments with different power bases that might be avoided with a more formal, written policy.

In defense of the unwritten nature of the policy, however, a dean stated:

> I find the unwritten, more informal process to be just fine, frankly. My sense is that on many of these things, which become clothed and wrapped, in a lot of judgments where peoples' egos are at stake that sometimes is best. Laws and rules can only go so far because people will still circumvent them. So it is much better to go one on one and use moral persuasion on people. . . . Now, when things don't work out people will scream, "Well, if it were only written down." That's not why it doesn't work out. It doesn't work because it's fated and the relationships and the personalities aren't going to work out and no rules or laws written down are going to make that happen. These are humans that have to get along. So long as there is an understanding of a policy and as long as it becomes more routinized, it's not viewed as exceptional or an unusual request, then it comes down to accommodating for people and do we want both these people. I like it that way.

Concluding Comment

While no one formula exists to help institutions create a formal procedure for hiring an accompanying spouse or partner, the following steps seem to be followed by most institutions that have such policies. First, make the initial candidate aware that the university has a formal dual-career hiring process. Second, contact the spouse or partner to gather information about objectives and qualifications (this usually involves obtaining the partner's vita). Third, apprise the relevant dean and vice president of the situation. Fourth, distribute the vita to the appropriate faculty, administrators, and human resources people. These steps are undertaken to determine if there may be a fit between the accompanying partner and a receiving academic unit and if there is a basis for proceeding with an interview. Next, the chair of the receiving department consults with the department's search advisory committee (or its equivalent) to review the vita, discuss the person's qualifications, and determine how they fit with departmental goals. If the outcome is negative, the process is discontinued. But if it seems positive, then the department interviews the accompanying partner to determine if the person has "sufficiently high achievements and/or potential to have made the short list for a position in the unit if the position had been advertised" and "has sufficiently high achievement and/or potential that the receiving department would desire to retain the individual even if the marriage or partnership dissolves." Assuming the answer to these questions is yes, then the process continues. The next step is discussions between the departments involved (both the one seeking the initial hire and the one willing to hire the accompanying partner). Among other things, the interested parties discuss funding the position and whether funding arrangements should change over time (if funding for the second position is to be shared). Further, the departments discuss whether the position offered is to be a term appointment (with the term specified) or a tenure-track position. At the stage where all parties are in agreement (including all relevant department chairs, deans, and vice presidents), a proposal is made to the provost. The proposal might include a request for up to one-third of the second hire's salary for up to three years. Assuming a positive outcome from all these steps, an offer would be sent to both the initial hire and the accompanying partner specifying the necessary conditions of employment for both. Once the partner joins the receiving department, he or she is to be treated the same as any other employee of the same rank and status in terms of merit review, promotion and tenure, working conditions, and so on.

For many dual-career academics, a tenure-track position for an accompanying spouse or partner is the most desired form of accommodation. It is also the rarest, most complicated, and most controversial. It is rare because so few academic institutions have created procedures for creating such positions. And even where such procedures exist, factors such as luck, timing, and cooperation, combined with the needs of an academic unit and the qualifications of the spouse or partner, must be aligned before such a position could be granted. Granting a tenure-track line to an accompanying spouse or partner has also created the most controversy among academics, since it brings with it worries about the quality of the hire, about eroding faculty autonomy, about equity, affirmative action, and fairness, and about strategic planning and resource allocation. While the relatively limited number of such positions granted should alleviate the backlash against dual-career hiring policies, the heightened attention given to them seems to fan the flames of discontent. The following chapter discusses each of these concerns in some detail.

9 | Common Concerns about Dual-Career Hiring Practices

There is little disagreement among academic couples that finding satisfying employment at the same institution, or at least at institutions close together, is ideal. In some circumstances, colleges and universities will find it advantageous to accommodate couples and partners. If the accommodation is successful, the institution will likely reap the benefits of improved recruitment and retention, have two happy, productive employees, and be viewed as family friendly. Yet the decision to accommodate is not an easy one. Typically, institutions weighing this decision worry about the fairness of accommodating spouses or partners of faculty members, the legality of such accommodations, the fear of diluting faculty quality, the implications for a unit's overall personnel needs, and maintaining faculty autonomy in hiring.

Some of these concerns are practical, and some arise from seemingly incompatible institutional and individual commitments. In this chapter we discuss these important concerns and explore some of the implications of possible resolutions. We draw on the relevant literature, our survey, and the case studies we conducted. We do not have the answers, but we believe that if institutions are to move toward satisfactory solutions to the growing problem of dual-career academic couples, they will have to address these key concerns.

Is Dual-Career Accommodation Fair?

As institutions of higher education consider whether to engage in dual-career accommodations of any kind, they are likely to hear questions concerning the fairness of doing so. In the hiring practices of colleges and universities until the 1960s, discrimination based on gender, ethnicity, and religion was common, and cronyism and nepotism were none too rare (Caplow and McGee 1958). The now familiar approach to hiring, including the public advertising of positions, reference checking, campus interview, and so forth, was intended to thwart discrimination and favoritism and thereby advance the principle of fairness. Dual-career policies, which some see as challenging this core principle, have met with strong opposition, as suggested by the following quotations from a colloquy in the *Chronicle of Higher Education* in 2000.

Although having a spouse nearby is definitely preferable, the preferential hiring of them by universities is wrong. The university should pick the best candidate for the job. As a single person, about to enter an academic job search, I feel very strongly about this.

Single male, 27, seeks "academic star" for marriage, good times, and possible help gaining full-time employment. . . . Come on people. Give me a break. The academic market is a jungle. Many single people cannot find jobs, so why would anyone expect it to be easy for couples to find jobs at the same institution? The argument that "a happy professor is a good professor" is just silly. If colleges were really worried about the happiness of those who teach students, we wouldn't have the abusive adjunct system we currently have.

The notion of preference for spouses seems an antiquated idea that endorses a certain very old fashioned family structure and value. Who decides what family structure an institution should support? When does "preference" become "nepotism"? Is spouse preference fair to people like me whose personal and professional struggles combined are substantive, complicated, and burdensome?

Under no circumstances should preferential treatment be given to academic spouses. I have seen several cases where a male faculty member was sought after so badly that another faculty position opening suddenly "materialized" to hire his spouse. If the spouse is that good, she should be able to compete for the position on her own merits. I find it extremely distasteful when universities manufacture positions for the favored few.

When the institution makes itself responsible for the family members it takes on a role that is neither appropriate nor financially supportable. Isn't it time that colleges and universities stopped being held accountable for anything except higher education and research? Why should a potential faculty member feel that his/her spouse is entitled to a job at the same institution? Do spouses of employees in other venues routinely expect the employer to offer them positions?

Analyzing these responses, one is struck by the different ways individuals perceive dual-career accommodations to be unfair. To describe their objection to such policies, they use words such as "nepotism," "favoritism," "discrimination," and "unfair entitlement." Clearly, many in academe believe that institutions should not accommodate dual-career academic couples—especially when the accommodation involves creating a tenure-track position for the accompanying spouse or partner. The objections to such policies vary. Some believe that dual-career accommodations unfairly disadvantage those who are single; others believe that academic institutions should not be catering to the needs of some faculty members while neglecting the equally pressing needs of others. But the basic question in regard to fairness is, Why should an individual be given special consideration simply because he or she is married to or partnered with another academic?

During our interviews, no respondents expressed the personal belief that dual-career accommodation is unfair in principle. This finding is predictable, since we interviewed only administrators and faculty who were at institutions that were making efforts to accommodate academic couples and who either had been accommodated or had participated in making an accommodation. It would have been surprising if they had said they thought their own policies or practices were unfair. However, they did describe many of their colleagues as being predisposed to believe that dual-career hiring is unfair in ways mirrored in the Chronicle colloquy cited above. Evidence of these views came from the hostility and stigmatizing that many of the accommodated spouses and partners felt from some of their departmental colleagues for having "received a position via an irregular route."

Questions about fairness were raised by some faculty who had been accommodated in ways they deemed inappropriate or inadequate. In particular, when accompanying spouses or partners were placed in temporary positions, as at Heartland University, they were likely to feel they had been treated unfairly—especially if a full-time position did not materialize quickly. We found this to be so even though couples had been told that there was no guarantee of a more permanent position. Some couples we interviewed believed that during the initial hire's interview they had been given false hope that a position would become available for the accompanying spouse. This was a particularly frustrating situation for both members of the couple and created some resentment. Even couples who themselves have opted to share a single position, as described in chapter 6, may perceive unfairness. The institution has two faculty members filling a single position, and their combined effort will typically exceed 100 percent time. Eventually they may feel frustrated by their single shared salary and their limited opportunities for advancement relative to faculty in "regular" positions. Though they asked to share a position, they still feel the accommodation is not always fair.

Academic couples who received no offers of assistance from their institutions may also perceive dual-career accommodations as unfair. As discussed earlier, many dual-career accommodation policies, especially those that involve granting tenure-track positions to the partners of initial hires, are not written or publicly advertised. Not every hire with an academic spouse or partner is offered an accommodation. Many institutions have policies that apply only to those being actively recruited. Faculty who were already employed before the policy was created, or who married after they came to the institution, tend to think the policy is unfair. Why, they asked, should these newer faculty receive special consideration merely because they were married at the time they were seeking employment?

Stated simply, many in higher education believe that dual-career accommodations thwart standardized hiring practices, advantaging those who are married or partnered over others who are also seeking employment but lack the connection to a sought-after significant other. Typically, these faculty consider all opportunity hires to be unfair. In a tight academic labor market and in times of fiscal constraint, offering an academic position, even a temporary one, to someone because he or she is married to or partnered with someone—even if the person is fully qualified—means that others will likely lose this opportunity for employment. Perceptions of fairness are relative, however. From the perspective of a couple seeking employment, the odds of finding two academic positions close to one another are poor enough to make it highly unlikely without some assistance. These faculty ask why they should be disadvantaged in their search for academic work solely because they have chosen other academics as their life partners.

It is not our purpose here to argue that dual-career accommodation is fair in principle. However, broad social changes that began occurring in the 1960s lead us to question the idea that fairness in hiring *requires* disregarding individuals' marital or partner status. Before large numbers of women began having careers of their own, the social expectation was that a woman would move to accommodate her husband's job. Relatively few couples can now live on just one income, and as it happens, academics often choose other academics as their life partners. Also, that women academics are more likely than their male counterparts to be married to other academics is another "fairness" factor that colleges and universities ought to take into account as they strive for a more equitable gender balance among their faculty. Given these realities, it is time, we think, to question what "fairness" might mean in this changed context.

If an institution chooses to consider hiring accompanying spouses or partners, it is surely going to have to wrestle with the perceived fairness of that policy. There will be critics who will always believe that the basis of the policy is flawed and creates inequities. However, the means by which the college or university carries out its dual-career policy can mitigate some complaints. Specifically, the more the policy is regularized, advertised as available, and known by those doing the hiring, the less likely it is to be seen as unfair.

Are Dual-Career Accommodation Policies Legal?

The legality of dual-career hiring policies has been questioned by academic administrators, and many fear that such policies will lead to lawsuits by individuals claiming that an institution unfairly discriminated against them in hiring. In our survey of provosts, as well as in our case study interviews, we were struck by the variety of perceptions regarding the legal status of dual-career hiring policies. Hence in this section we provide a layperson's guide to some of the concerns raised by those considering dual-career hiring policies. Our discussion does not address specific case law, nor does it make distinctions between guidelines and policies for public and private institutions. Indeed, most of the discussion is more relevant to public institutions than to private ones, since the hiring policies and practices of private institutions tend to be relatively idiosyncratic.

Nepotism Rules

According to Shoben (1997), dual-career hiring policies, by definition, "are a form of nepotism because an individual receives a benefit in employment by virtue of a familial relationship with an employee." She adds, "It doesn't matter whether that benefit is a full academic appointment or something else; any kind of benefit premised upon a familial relationship suffices to make the practice nepotistic" (237). Perhaps this is why many respondents to our survey, as discussed in chapter 2, cited the presence of campus or statewide nepotism policies as a justification for not having a dual-career hiring policy. Any discussion of the "legality" of nepotism policies must consider that such policies are typically institutionally based rather than legal strictures. As such, there is nothing illegal per se about nepotistic hiring practices. Nonetheless, several respondents to our survey stated explicitly that they do not hire spouses of employees, especially in the same academic department, because of institutionally based nepotism policies. The central concern expressed in the survey was that family members should not supervise each other or influence decisions about such matters as tenure or merit raises for another family member. Approximately twenty institutions said their nepotism policies prohibited them from hiring the spouses or partners of academics. Some administrators at public institutions explained their lack of a dual-career accommodation policy in terms of their states' rules on conflict of interest. At one institution, for instance, the provost wrote:

> We have a statement in our Conflict of Interest Policy regarding members of the same family. The college does not recommend that members of the same family be employed in the same department or office. However, the college does not prohibit employment of family members in the same department or administrative unit, provided that neither family member participates in making decisions or recommendations specifically affecting appointment, retention, work assignments, promotion, demotion or salary of another family member.

While some concern over nepotism clearly remains, nepotism rules are becoming less prevalent in higher education, in large part because such rules have been implicated in discrimination against women. Historically, it has been the wife of an academic who is the accompanying spouse, and nepotism policies have often precluded employment in academia for these women. Heightened awareness of this outcome, coupled with some successful lawsuits, has led increasing numbers of academic institutions to abandon their nepotism policies in favor of dual-career hiring policies. From a nepotism policy standpoint, as long as the members of an academic couple do not participate in decisions about tenure, promotion, merit pay, and such regarding their spouses or partners, most institutions would be safe in making a dual-career accommodation. Further, as long as these policies do not lead to discrimination against individuals based on age, race, ethnicity, religion, or gender, there is nothing specifically illegal about them, despite the negative association with nepotism.

Perceived Discrimination

Most campus equal opportunity offices warn against asking questions about marital status during interviews. From this fact one might assume that marital status is a protected class. This is not the case, however. The "don't ask" rule is rooted in concerns about discriminating against individuals based on gender—a federally protected classification. The fear is that if one learns that a woman has a spouse, then members of a search committee may be tempted to withhold a job offer based on stereotypical assumptions about her commitment to the job. They could assume, for example, that a woman is the secondary wage earner in a family and may need the job less than a man who is the primary wage earner. Or they may assume that she is more likely to leave to follow her husband should he accept a job elsewhere. They may assume that she is likely to have a lower commitment to work than a man would because of her responsibilities at home (which typically fall disproportionately to women). Not knowing the marital status of potential employees protects those on search committees from making hiring decisions based on stereotypes and thus helps the decision makers to avoid discriminatory hiring practices. Asking questions about marital status, even if the search committee does not use such information in the hiring decision, may open the institution to claims of gender discrimination from those not hired.

Nondiscriminatory Hiring Practices

Assumptions aside, institutions seeking to accommodate dual-career couples should be mindful of federal and state laws regarding nondiscriminatory hiring practices. Dual-career policies cannot discriminate against individuals based on age, gender, race or ethnicity, national origin, religion, disability, or veteran status. A variety of federal laws explicitly protect members of these demographic classifications from employment discrimination. Specifically, the Fourteenth Amendment to the Constitution and the statutes that extend and enforce it, like Title 9, require equal protection for protected classifications as well as due process. It is important to note that protection against discrimination is extended to anyone within the protected classification; for example, men and women and whites and minorities are offered equal protection under the law. The general rule is that hiring institutions need to treat groups in the same way. There are exceptions, of course. Affirmative action is the main one, since it passes the compelling state interest test: that is, the state can go against its own general rule if it has a very good reason for doing so. In looking at the Fourteenth Amendment and its application to hiring policies, one can claim discrimination by two paths. First, one can claim disparate treatment (overt racism, for example). Or one can claim disparate impact, when a neutral policy has a discriminatory effect.

On the surface, a dual-career hiring policy is not likely to lead to discriminatory hiring practices based on these protected classifications. Depending on how the policy is implemented, there is no reason to believe that any one gender or any one race would benefit at the expense of others. That is, as long as the dual-career policy is not used solely to hire individuals of a certain gender or race, then academic institutions will generally find themselves protected against lawsuits from those claiming such discrimination. Further, if an institution has a policy that it follows explicitly in hiring an accompanying spouse or partner, the institution should be protected from claims of discrimination, because marital status is not a legally protected classification.

Although marital status is not a federally protected classification, a few states do have laws protecting individuals from such discrimination; but these laws are rare. What is more common is for institutions themselves to proclaim in their hiring documents that they do not discriminate based on marital status. Such claims are legally binding and obligate the institution to make sure that their hiring policies are not discriminatory in this regard. In other words, institutions are responsible for upholding their own rules and can be found liable for failing to do so. Having an institutional statement forbidding discrimination based on marital status does not preclude an institution's having a dual-career hiring policy. But such a statement would require that its implementation—as suggested by the overall hiring practices of the institution—not lead to discriminatory hiring patterns by marital status.

While it is usually not illegal to discriminate against individuals based on marital status, one may decide it is better to avoid the whole question of dual-career hiring by not offering a position to anyone who requests an accommodation for his or her spouse or partner. One might just decide it would be easier to hire someone who is single. Such a decision would be problematic from a number of perspectives. First, institutions that refuse to hire a member of a dual-career couple may miss out on the most qualified applicant. Further, an institution that opts out of hiring such a candidate might find itself inadvertently discriminating against individuals based on gender. This is in large part because women academics are more likely than their male counterparts to be married to other academics. As such, institutionals that avoid the dual-career question altogether are at risk of engaging in gender discrimination. What we want to make clear is that it is not illegal to engage in dual-career accommodations if they are conducted correctly, but that it would be unwise to discriminate against a person because he or she is married or partnered.

Requirements regarding Open Searches

Generally speaking, academic institutions must conduct open searches in order to comply with Executive Order 11246. This federal law requires organizations (including colleges and universities) that have fifty or more employees and more than $50,000 in government contracts to establish written affirmative action plans and to make special efforts to correct the effects of past and present discrimination. Chapter 60 of this law specifies the procedures that academic institutions must follow to be in compliance with affirmative action and equal opportunity hiring. These procedures fall into three broad categories: outreach and recruitment; monitoring the hiring process to make sure it is nondiscriminatory; and setting goals based on an examination of job group (e.g., engineering faculty) in relation to availability of women and minorities.

The Office of Federal Contract Compliance Programs (OFCCP), under the Department of Labor, is charged with ensuring that colleges and universities comply with these procedures. The OFCCP audits federal contractors, including colleges and universities, to assess their compliance. Institutions that fail to comply with the regulations in Chapter 60 can lose federal funds. Note that the OFCCP has no official policy regarding dual-career hiring policies. Aside from the OFCCP audits, an individual job applicant who believed that an academic institution engaged in discriminatory hiring practices could file a complaint with the federal or state Equal Employment Opportunity Commission (EEOC). The EEOC would investigate the complaint to determine its legitimacy and take action, if appropriate. To date, however, there have been no formal complaints to the EEOC by job applicants about dual-career policies, and therefore such policies have not come under government scrutiny. Complainants also have the right to file individual lawsuits against hiring institutions if their EEOC investigations were not completed in a timely manner or failed to resolve the problem in a satisfactory way.

While colleges and universities must follow these hiring policies, they are certainly within their legal rights to conduct closed searches in certain circumstances, especially if the situation furthers an institutional goal and is in accord with institutional policies. At most colleges and universities, those wishing to proceed with a closed search must fill out some sort of waiver form that is reviewed by the institution's equal opportunity officer and by the chief academic officer.

Legal Lessons across Cases

The most important lesson to remember with regard to dual-career accommodations is that institutions that follow their own rules and do not act in an arbitrary or capricious manner are likely to avoid legal trouble. Nonetheless, respondents at all the institutions in our study that created faculty positions for accompanying spouses or partners were concerned about the implications of forgoing open searches, in part because doing so seemed at odds with Chapter 60 of Executive Order 11246. This concern led all of them to develop guidelines to safeguard against violating legal mandates. While they addressed this concern somewhat differently, the following list represents the basic approach taken to ensure compliance with Chapter 60.

- Departments wishing to hire an accompanying spouse or partner are required to submit a form to the Equal Opportunity Office requesting a waiver of an open search. In all cases, the form asks departments to justify why a regular search is being circumscribed. When relevant, departments are asked to address how the particular hire will affect affirmative action goals, either positively or negatively.
- Except for not advertising the job opening, the search procedure for hiring an accompanying spouse is the same as that followed in any search. The vita is examined, references are checked, the candidate comes to campus for an interview and job talk, and the department votes on whether to hire the person. As several respondents explained, the procedure is "like a regular search, but with an *n* of one."
- In cases where the accompanying spouse is a woman or a person of color, forgoing an open search is easier because the hire will typically advance affirmative action goals. In contrast, if the accompanying spouse is a white male, then the institution's affirmative action goals may impede waiving the search. Ironically, such a decision can work against affirmative action hiring when the leading spouse is a women or a person of color. Given this complexity, administrators need to carefully consider requests for dual-career hiring in light of their affirmative action goals.
- The institutions in our case studies were all aware that while their dual-career hiring policy could be used to help them hire affirmatively, they needed to avoid favoring one race or gender in hiring overall. (As noted

above, a dual-career hiring policy that favors any one group, whether it is women or men, minorities or whites, would be subject to claims of discrimination and possible lawsuits.) As a result, the institutions enacted their dual-career hiring policies in ways that would be perceived as gender and race neutral.

Other Legal Concerns

While a search of the legal index Westlaw reveals no lawsuits brought against colleges or universities for dual-career hiring practices, there are still some important legal issues to be considered. As we examined the spouse and partner hiring processes followed by the academic institutions in our study, it became clear that because many of them are not conducting an open search (they are not advertising positions), they could be questioned during an OFCCP audit or if an EEOC complaint was filed. When asked about the legality of such policies, program officers at OFCCP said they would look at dual-career hiring case by case. They stated that if an institution could demonstrate that it was meeting its affirmative action goals and that it was generally making a good-faith effort to have a broad applicant pool for most of its searches, then the office might look more favorably on the few hiring situations in which a closed search was initiated. If the institution had a poor record of affirmative action hiring or of having open searches, however, then a spouse or partner hire would be more suspect. The risk of losing federal funds in such circumstances is small, but it is generally better to be extra cautious and to take even small risks into consideration.

Universities and colleges that choose to forgo an open search, whether it is for a spouse or partner hire or for some other purpose, would be wise to ensure that their decision making could be deemed "reasonable" by an outside body, including the courts and federal regulatory agencies. Since what might be considered "reasonable" is not codified, they might want to ask questions like those asked by administrators at Heartland: How will this closed search affect affirmative action goals at department and institution levels? How scarce are our resources? If we make this hire, will it slow progress toward meeting goals for affirmative hiring? Looking at the situation holistically, would we be better served by hiring candidate X, even if hiring his or her spouse doesn't help us to achieve our goals? Take, as an example, the following scenario: An institution offers a position to a female engineer, but she will come only if her husband, a chemist, is also hired. The question to be asked from an affirmative action stance is, Does the advantage of hiring the woman in engineering outweigh what may be perceived as the potential disadvantage of hiring another white male in chemistry?

Institutions that choose to hire spouses through a more regular search (they advertise positions) are less likely to face problems from federal regulators, but they are more apt to be sued for discrimination by an applicant who did not get the position, especially if the search was not "really open." If an institution conducts an open search and a spouse prevails, then someone else could claim discrimination in hiring. To win the lawsuit, however, the complainant would have to demonstrate that the dual-career hiring policy had a disparate impact based on race or gender. This would be difficult to prove because, on its face, it does not appear that dual-career hiring policies favor one gender or race over another. Nonetheless, it is unwise for institutions to claim to conduct an open search when the outcome is predetermined.

It seems unlikely that closed searches in which the institutional dual-career accommodation policy is followed (when a search waiver has been obtained) that result in the employment of a spouse or partner will generate lawsuits. According to Elinor Schroeder, professor of law at the University of Kansas, this can be explained by the fact that there is no clear victim when an institution conducts this type of "search." There is no person who can easily claim discrimination when a spouse is hired through a closed process because that person would not have applied for the job in the first place. And clearly there would be no way to judge his or her qualifications against those of the individual who received the position.

To recapitulate, worries about nepotism and affirmative action aside, dual-career accommodation policies have not led to lawsuits in higher education. Safeguards against lawsuits include ensuring that policies do not have a disparate impact based on gender or race, applying the policies fairly and across the board, and keeping good records about who is being accommodated. Given the changing nature of law and idiosyncrasies within states and institutions, we recommend consulting the university's equal opportunity officer and general counsel before implementing a dual-career policy.

Finding the Best: Perceptions of Faculty Quality

No concern is more central to dual-career accommodations, or any opportunity hire for that matter, than faculty quality. Its centrality is reflected in an equity survey recently completed at the University of Kansas. A major finding is that many faculty members believe that opportunity hires of all sorts are held to lower standards than faculty hired through regular searches (ku.edu/ffiprovost/equity%20study/index.html). These professors thought such hires reduced the quality of the faculty and, in turn, the quality of the institution. This view is rooted in the belief that traditional faculty searches (at least at the junior level) should be open contests and that by nature open contests in which all are invited to apply yield the best candidates. Given this view, a "search" with only one candidate is bound to raise questions. How can we be sure this is the best candidate when there are no others to compare? Shouldn't colleges and universities hire the most qualified faculty regardless of whether these faculty have academic spouses or partners?

Here we try to shed some light on institutional understandings of faculty quality in relation to dual-career accommodation. Using data from our case study sites, we look at how administrators and faculty address the issue. Among these administrators and faculty there was a great deal of concern over quality, in particular over how institutions could ensure high-quality faculty while also accommodating dual-career couples. That said, while the view was not unanimous, most respondents at the case study sites believed that, if used judiciously, dual-career accommodations can improve overall institutional quality by attracting and retaining high-quality faculty.

Hilltop University

Although faculty quality is an overriding concern in spouse and partner hires at "Hilltop University," it is not a contentious one. (See chapter 3 for a fuller description of "Hilltop University.") We believe this lack of contention results because the policy is used selectively, departments have the final say in hiring, and the faculty search and selection process for spouse and partner hires follows very closely the sponsored contest mobility model that characterizes faculty hires in general at Hilltop. That is, characteristics such as the prestige of one's degree-granting institution and the reputation of one's mentor are factors in all hiring decisions whether through a closed or an open search. It also helps that faculty members at Hilltop seem to have a good sense of what excellence or quality is in their context. Here are some factors that have minimized disputes about faculty quality at Hilltop.

First, the policy is used selectively. Department chairs seemed hesitant to consider a spouse or partner hire if the initial hire was not the top candidate, whether the initial hire was a senior or junior person. For example, one department chair explained, "I probably wouldn't have done it [spousal hire for an assistant professor]—well, we don't make offers unless we are pretty excited about the candidate." In fact, he went on to tell us that another college had tried to get his department to put up most of the salary to hire a spouse, but "they [the initial hire's college] said, 'It's only an assistant professor and to be honest, he's not even our top candidate.' I was, at that point, a little put out that I'd gone through all the motions because I expected I wouldn't be asked to do this unless they were pretty serious about a spousal hire." Thus, part of the unwritten practice surrounding spouse and partner hires at Hilltop seemed to be that if a college or department requests an accommodation, they must be serious, and the initial candidate must be top flight.

Second, it became very clear to us that departments that would "receive" a spouse or partner have the ultimate say in the hiring decision. Again, this seemed to be well accepted among deans and department chairs. (In fact, we noted remarkable collegiality among deans and department chairs at this large research university.) Although there was wide variation and lack of clarity in whether "official searches" took place for spouse or partner hires, the procedure in general followed that of a regular search, even if a search with only one candidate. One department chair explained how the process worked in his department, which was (with minor variations) followed in all the departments we visited:

> What happened in X was: [The chair] called me. He said, "Our top prospect has a spouse who is a psychologist and would we look at her vita?" She happened to be an African American. It was a wonderful vita; great letters, and we were enthusiastic. It would have been in the developmental psych area and they [the faculty] voted unanimously to recommend to the budget council [to fund a position]. Their [budget council's] recommendation was to bring the person in for an interview. In the end, it turned out that there was a fundamental mismatch between the candidate and the department. . . . I got a message from the dean, who said he'd like to see this happen but I'm not going to do this unilaterally and there was a very strong consensus among people—most of the department was at the talk—and almost everyone felt the same way. This was just not an appropriate fit.

The other chair involved in the incident described above emphasized that essentially the same procedure was followed in his department, which had been asked to look at the spouse of a scientist from a very good science department. The chair made some rather telling comments about this particular request. First he said, "We looked at her stuff and we think it is odd that this person is at an Ivy League university and has almost no publications and it is amazing that she is there and we haven't heard of her." The implication was that if this person was "good enough" for a place like Hilltop then the faculty would already have been familiar with her work. This particular request eventually died because recruitment of the initial hire didn't work out. However, this department chair confirmed that if the recruitment effort had been successful, the following would have occurred: "If it had worked out we would have looked at her vita and we'd have discussed it. It if were a senior person hopefully it would be somebody we'd heard of. Or somebody would have read some or been aware of her research. [Assuming she met the standards] it would be like any other appointment. . . . We'd have to bring them in for an interview. We aren't going to appoint someone without going through the process."

A dean commented that she always wanted to be helpful, and she gave the following as an example: "[When another unit approached me], I gave the vita to the chair of the department and said that we were trying to be helpful. . . . My attitude is that I always try to be helpful, but I also don't force anyone on a department."

There have been a number of successful dual-career hires at Hilltop, and these cases are well known on campus. Several of the initial hires had been at Hilltop for some time. In one case an academic department got a very well known economics professor for one-third of his normal salary because they agreed to hire him as an accompanying spouse (his wife, an assistant professor, was an initial hire in another department). In another case the woman in a dual-career couple was not happy in her present position within the institution, so she met with the faculty in another unit and was hired by them. Her new dean said: "We won big time." These "internal" cases worked somewhat differently, but it was clear that negotiations and the receiving department's stamp of approval were necessary before an accompanying spouse would be hired.

The examples above illustrate the sponsored contest nature of these appointments. Qualifications of the spouse or partner are judged in much the same way as those of the initial hire: by prestige of the graduate institution, by whether the faculty have heard of the candidates' work, by their references, by reputation, and by fit with the needs of the department. As one department chair indicated: "There are a huge number of candidates but a small number of really great candidates, and we go after what we consider to be the really top people that everyone else will be going after."

Our interviews included only those faculty at Hilltop who had been accommodated through the dual-career policy and faculty in departments who had voted on spouse and partner hires. Thus we do not know how the faculty at large views the issue in terms of faculty quality. Yet it seemed clear that quality was not a contentious issue at Hilltop; there was a clear understanding within units of what constituted quality, and control of spouse and partner hires seemed to be firmly in the hands of the faculty. Undoubtedly, the substantial financial commitment required of all three parties contributed to the caution with which Hilltop approached spouse and partner hires. Despite all this, several of the spousal hires did say they had to work hard to be fully accepted by their departments.

Heartland University

The dual-career accommodation policy at "Heartland University" is also intended to help the institution attract the very highest quality faculty it can in its competition with other elite universities. (See chapter 3 for a fuller description of "Heartland University.") These faculty are not too likely to be Nobel laureates; rather, they are younger scholars with "great potential." How faculty quality is understood at Heartland is illuminated most clearly by the faculty fellows component of its dual-career accommodation policy. As discussed in chapter 5, this component is designed primarily to serve as a recruiting tool for junior faculty. Briefly, the Faculty Fellows Program provides spouses and partners with one-year (in most cases) appointments in teaching, research, or administration, office space, and some benefits. The fellowship is intended to help individuals in the short term as they look for a full-time position at Heartland or at another institution in the area.

Given the relatively low stakes (recall that the Faculty Fellows Program provides for only one year, non-tenure-track appointments), it is at first somewhat surprising that the issue of quality at Heartland appears to be contentious, and attitudes are varied. Some of the deans and department chairs recognized the need to adopt more flexible hiring practices for the Faculty Fellows Program while maintaining the same levels of quality as perceived to emerge from regular searches. Some respondents clearly thought candidates should be evaluated just as if they were tenure-track faculty, whereas others described the fellows as glorified graduate assistants.

How might one explain the various understandings about what constitutes faculty quality? Heartland is a research university torn between serving the state's population and striving to be nationally known for high-quality research. At the same time, its geographic location makes it difficult to attract faculty stars. Concepts of quality may also be contentious because the Faculty Fellows Program is invoked frequently, and there is considerable dissatisfaction from various fronts with the temporary status of these non-tenure-track positions. One chair commented: "Quality would begin to be threatened if you always did it [used tenure-track positions] to accommodate spouses." This same chair said, "I have always insisted on two criteria when we review one of these things [request for a faculty fellows appointment]. One of them is the person's record; whatever state they are at, the question is, Are they of the quality that they can be a tenured faculty at a research I university? And we won't bend on that. The second one, which is a little dicier, is, Do we need a person in this area?"

A major concern about dual-career accommodations at Heartland is that forgoing an open search would reduce the likelihood that a real star would apply for the position. In other words, individuals were concerned that if you hired whoever you had available, even if they were very good, you would never know whom you might have gotten if the search had been open. As one dean explained:

> If you, in fact, bend on quality and take somebody who is kind of good, without going through a national search, you may not be getting as good a person as you can. There are still pockets on this campus that are not willing to do this for that reason—because they believe in the really open search, partly for political reasons, and partly because they believe that is what is going to get you the top faculty. You never know when you agree to a real affirmative action hire [or any opportunity hire], that you are going to get the best person you would get if you had advertised.

The overriding fear of whom you were missing out on by "settling" for a spouse or partner hire—or any target hire, even someone in a temporary position—was palpable at Heartland. We attribute this concern in large part to the fact that this institution, like many others, is striving to be more prestigious.

This fear had an effect on the hiring of individuals in the Faculty Fellows Program. Although a formal search procedure is not followed, faculty members are usually involved to some extent in the appointment of the fellow, and there is a high level of concern about quality. In almost all cases a vita is requested, and sometimes teaching evaluations and references as well. In many cases the individual seeking a faculty fellows appointment is interviewed. This is done to ensure that the applicant is good enough.

In determining whether to accommodate a faculty fellow, many departments look both at the academic record and at the department's need for the person's services. Several units, while employing high standards in decisions to appoint fellows, seemed to be almost grateful for the opportunity. All units agreed that people were seldom rejected for one-year appointments. One dean reflected that, in the case of the Faculty Fellows Program, "You have to take each case on its own merits and needs, and you just try to create an opportunity if you can. . . . You have got to be prepared to make some decisions, which oftentimes aren't very popular. By that I mean, if you've got somebody that you really want and there is this dual-career issue, and you have to find a way to get the person, you may only have a couple of opportunities." On the other hand, he said, "We don't hire people if faculty don't want them. I don't know of a single case where we told a department that they had to take somebody. We would never do that. They go through a process just like a normal hire with a pool of one. . . . That is our only way to ensure that we are going to get some kind of acceptable fit. I think we have made some very good hires that we could never have made otherwise."

This same person expanded on conceptions of faculty quality: "Higher education has drifted into what I think is a very destructive definition of quality, which is all gate-keeping based. We define quality in terms of the height of the hurdles that people had to go over to get jobs. It is almost as if being proactive is . . . like a lapse of quality. Because you violated this process, which is set up with all kinds of barriers and hurdles this became your definition of quality." Further, he noted that anyone who needs help or assistance of any sort is viewed as having weaknesses. He explained, "We have a large number of faculty who would complain if we went out and hired a Nobel laureate without a search because we didn't go through the process. It puts a heavy constraint on how much accommodation you can do."

Another dean echoed this ambivalence somewhat sarcastically: "We are going to do it the way we've always done it even if it doesn't work. . . . It is surprising that even though here [through an opportunity hire] is a chance for a department to get a really good person someone will say: 'This isn't what you are supposed to do.'" He continued: "The 'right' way is interesting. You put an ad in the *Chronicle* and you wait for people to apply. No other business would try to improve itself that way. Any other business would go out to find the very best people they could find. The traditional process may be fine at the beginning assistant professor level. I think it works here. Right now we are looking for a senior person in math education. There's no prayer that person is going to apply to an ad in the *Chronicle*. The people we want are well-established where they are."

Although one dean distinguished clearly between evaluating those in the Faculty Fellows Program and those in tenure-track positions, there was considerable confusion evident in our interviews at Heartland. Many deans and chairs seemed to confuse the two, even though the faculty fellow appointment was for only one year, with no guarantees. As one dean stated, "I am committed to the dual-career program, the concept of attracting faculty by helping in the relationships with the spouse. I do think that if we are going to offer them a tenure-track position or even a permanent staff position, that we need to use the same kind of evaluative tools as we use for anyone else."

Faculty reactions to accompanying spouses also suggest something about the institution's perceptions of quality. At Heartland, there was quite a lot of concern over acceptance of faculty fellows. One dean said, "My perception would be that initially there might be some carryover. They say, 'Okay, someone got that position that really was not the person we would have hired.' For the majority it is how the person performs and then it goes away. But I'm sure there are always a few who don't forget." A faculty member confirmed this: "There remains an aura of being second rate—this indefinable something that one isn't up to snuff because one doesn't have a tenured position."

Several of the Heartland administrators we spoke with argued for a different way of finding high-quality faculty. One associate dean argued that spouse and partner hires will not occur if the "national search" approach to finding the best faculty is adhered to inflexibly. She said, "If you don't have a process that permits this kind of appointment, that is, if departments are still thinking, 'Oh, we have to do a national search and pick the very best candidate from among the 300 applicants that we get, [then it is unlikely that even qualified spouses and partners will be hired]." She went on to describe an alternative approach to hiring faculty.

> Instead of rank ordering all of your candidates and looking for the very top that you do it by way of *satisficing*. Satisficing comes out of decision-making theory. What it involves is that you decide on your minimal criteria for the job and then you just make your cut and say that everyone above the line would be acceptable. You draw the line here and everyone who meets those criteria is equally satisfac-

tory. You don't do rank ordering. This would allow someone who is a dual-career partner to stand out. Because the way it is done now—if you do the rank ordering—then it is very unlikely statistically that your dual-career partner is going to end up one of the top three slots. [Dual-career hires are] an enormous problem because it goes against faculty culture so much.

It is safe to say that the concept of "satisficing" would be rejected by most institutions, even if this is what happens in many technically open searches. The idea of satisficing does not fit well with most people's understanding of quality and how it is found. Regardless of its actual outcome, the "open contest" is still thought essential to finding the most qualified applicant. Maintaining or raising the quality of Heartland and its faculty was of great concern to many we interviewed. How these concerns overlap and affect the hiring of dual-career couples will have a long-term impact on the sustainability of the institution's efforts at dual-career accommodation.

Riverdale University

Discussions with faculty and administrators at "Riverdale University" about the Bridge Program did not yield many comments about faculty quality. (See chapter 3 for a fuller description of "Riverdale University.") Perhaps this is because the Bridge Program, like the procedure followed at Hilltop, was used only selectively. And as at Hilltop, it was widely believed that having a dual-career hiring policy was more likely to raise the quality of the faculty at the university than to lower it. Nevertheless, faculty quality is perceived to be an important factor that must be maintained, especially in dual-career accommodations. According to one dean, people at Riverdale try hard to be receptive to dual-career hires. He stated, "It doesn't mean that the faculty will make any exceptions in terms of quality, but they will certainly at least have a look at the résumé . . . and if it looks like a reasonably good hire they will go ahead with it." This dean said that if someone contacted him about a spouse or partner accommodation, he would send the résumé to the appropriate department. The department would then evaluate the résumé, interview the person, and then, assuming the person was of "high quality," make an offer. Another dean confirmed this:

> Someone says to us, "We have a very good candidate; they have a trailing spouse, would you help?" And we say, "Send the résumé. We will look at it." If it comes to me I will send it to the appropriate school in engineering and they will look at

it. They will then take it to their faculty search committee, if there is one. If not, the head will look at it and maybe convene a group to see if they expect a retirement in the next couple of years. . . . It's a full interview. If they are anticipating an opening in the future, they are not likely to open up a full-advertised search. The procedure is the same. The faculty will look at the candidate and make the judgment, advise the head, etc. There are no exceptions made to the quality standard in the sense that you go through the same sort of review.

A critical part of this is "to build into the system a mechanism so that the faculty considering the trailing spouse has full input into the decision so [that] the trailing spouse, if hired, does indeed become a full-fledged colleague, not somebody who is there on the margin, somebody who, 'well, after six years they are out, we'll make life miserable for them so they quit.'" One administrator offered his definition of quality: "I think they know quality when they see it. Somebody who has a good start and has a lot of potential, who has ideas, energy, and ambition—the full package."

Yet the director of affirmative action complained that accompanying spouses are sometimes viewed as illegitimate:

One recognizes what one needs to do to attract a faculty member, but there is also the myopia of any institution where the department thinks they are hiring the talented person, the person they want, but however renowned the initial hire, the spouse can't be a worthy scholar. A department asks, "Would you consider X who is the spouse or partner of Y, whom we are really trying to recruit?" The department sometimes acts as if that is the last person in the world we want to hire because, surely, that person is often a woman. As institutions, we have to overcome this sense that the accompanying spouse cannot be the sort of scholar that we want to have in their own right.

Riverdale is in somewhat the same situation as Heartland in terms of recruiting faculty to a relatively rural area. However, Riverdale's faculty and administration share an understanding of what constitutes faculty quality. It was also clear that Riverdale believed it needed to recruit women and recognized that dual-career hiring would aid that effort.

Belle State University

At "Belle State University," there is no apparent disagreement over what constitutes faculty quality, and administrators state explicitly that they view dual-career accommodation as a means of ensuring quality. (See chapter 3 for a fuller description of "Belle State University.") It does so, they believe, by enabling the university to attract top-flight faculty who happen to have academic spouses. The assistant provost at the university clarified: "[When the question about a star's trailing spouse arises] I have said, 'Do whatever it takes to hire that faculty person onto the campus.' In one case it was all the way of creating a position in another department—a tenured position in which they interviewed the [accompanying] spouse." Here again, the assistant provost stressed that while she sees accommodation as a means of attracting the best and brightest, it is imperative that the accompanying spouse also be of high quality: "We [the Provost's Office] would never go to a department and tell them to hire a person just because they happened to be married to a person we want to hire. We obviously can't do that. They have to go through a process."

While Belle State had on rare occasion created a tenure-track position in order to attract an especially desirable new faculty member, that person's spouse would still go through a regular search. Rather than creating positions, though, as we discussed in chapter 5, the preferred approach to accommodation at Belle State is to hire accompanying spouses as visiting appointments. The Provost's Office explained: "The visiting appointment is much more convenient because it gives the [department where the accompanying spouse is placed for a limited term] an opportunity to meet and work with the individual and then make a decision or gives this person a chance to be in this area and find something else that might be better." In other words, lectureships and other short-term appointments are preferred at Belle State as a means of ensuring that faculty quality is maintained.

The Special Case of Faculty Stars

When considering faculty quality, efforts to hire academic stars deserve special mention. Even though dual-career accommodations at most institutions are possible for faculty at every rank, across the institutions in our study such accommodations were seen as somewhat less questionable in terms of quality when the initial hire was a recognized "star" in his or her field. In large part this is because of the leverage such a high-powered individual holds and because of the perceived value brought to the institution. It is also because many assume that "smart people marry other smart people." As a corollary, some assume that the spouse or partner of an exceptionally productive scholar is likely to also be of high quality. According to a department chair at Riverdale: "We hired an upper-level faculty member who would only come here if we were to give his spouse a position within our department. Fortunately, he had the right bargaining chips because she was exactly what we needed as well. . . . We were obviously a bit swayed to do this because we wanted to hire him so badly."

This department chair went on to explain that while he was motivated to pursue options for accommodating the star's wife, he also took steps to ensure that she too was well qualified. Similarly, the quality of the initial hire comes into play at Heartland when a request is made to hire an accompanying spouse or partner. As one chair said, "The dean has to be convinced that you, the faculty hire, are worth it so that they want to keep you and thus want to make your spouse happy. If the dean thinks you are not, then the funding falls through." At Belle State and Hilltop University as well, the higher the status and marketability of initial hires, the more likely the institution is to make accommodations for their spouses or partners. Based on the case studies, we conclude that quality of an accompanying spouse or partner is regarded differently depending on the quality of the initial hire.

At the same time, however, the accompanying spouse or partner of a highly sought-after academic may be perceived as merely benefiting from the mate's influence and not possessing the skills or attributes needed to make it alone. The "Matthew effect" as described by Merton (1988) comes into play here. The Matthew effect alludes to the biblical passage, "For whosoever hath, to him shall be given, and he shall have more abundance; but whosoever hath not, from him shall be taken away even that he hath" (Matt. 25:29). In terms of a dual-career accommodation, the Matthew effect suggests that the success of a spouse or partner of a prominent person is the direct result of the work of the more prominent member of the couple. In this case it is the accompanying spouse or partner who "hath not." The problem is exacerbated if both are in the same field or if they publish together, since many assume that the more senior member of the pair is responsible for the work. Clark and Corcoran's (1986) description of the "Salieri phenomenon" is also appropriate in terms of dual-career hiring. They suggest that just as the composer Antonio Salieri helped Mozart find employment, he also blocked Mozart's career progress. In a dual-career situation something similar occurs when the initial hire is of a higher status than his or her spouse or partner. Accommodating the initial hire may allow the spouse or partner to find work, but it may also thwart his or her career aspirations.

The gender of the initial hire is an important attribute to consider in discussions of faculty quality. Traditionally it is the woman who is the accompanying spouse or partner of an academic star. The stereotype is that the academic wife of an academic star is younger, less established, and riding on the coattails of her more accomplished husband. She may have potential as a scholar, but she will probably always be seen as being less qualified than she would appear if she were unattached. If she is hired into a tenure-track position, she is always likely to be perceived as having been granted a "favor" and to be undeserving of the position. When the accompanying spouse or partner is male, the situation is equally difficult. In this case the accompanying husband or partner is seen as riding on the skirt of his more accomplished wife—a scenario fraught with tension in our society. While we focus more on policy than on individual adaptation of the dual-career couple, it is important to note that, based on our interviews, when the accommodation is made to hire a man, the secondary hire's dissatisfaction is likely to be greater than if the secondary hire is a woman. This is especially true if the accommodation is temporary rather than a tenure-track position.

Reflections on Perceptions of Faculty Quality across Cases

The desire to hire the best faculty was evident at all our case study sites, but no one we spoke to suggested that accommodating spouses would necessarily interfere with this goal. In fact, accommodating dual-career couples—at least when one partner is near or at the top of his or her field and the other is also a viable candidate—was viewed as a means of enhancing faculty quality. In all the cases we examined, it was left to the receiving department to determine whether the accompanying spouse or partner was qualified for the position. In this regard, at these institutions dual-career accommodation is consistent with recognized principles of quality.

The institutions we studied seemed to have found ways to hire top-quality faculty and to accommodate at least some dual-career academics. This appears to call into question the notion that an open contest for positions is the only way to be sure of hiring high-quality faculty. Clearly, hiring someone merely because she or he is the partner of a desired candidate would tend to dilute faculty quality. But none of the institutions we are familiar with do so. In fact they go to considerable lengths to make sure that unqualified faculty are not hired, no matter how attractive their academic partners may be. This was the case for all types of accommodation, ranging from tenure track to short-term, adjunct positions.

What we conclude from our examination of case studies, survey, discussions, and review of the literature is that spouse and partner hires will tend to be less contentious when the same institutional processes and criteria for hiring are followed in both dual-career accommodations and regular hires and when spouse and partner hires are made selectively. The data from these cases do not address whether institutions of higher education can or should think differently about the procedure they use or the faculty they hire. In fact, we did not find much evidence of innovative thinking. Nor does the evidence from these cases suggest that we should.

Thus, many questions remain. Would institutions be better able to accommodate dual-career couples and opportunity hires and maintain quality if they relied on the principle of "satisficing" and invested in a more proactive human resource development model for assisting faculty? Would such an approach negatively affect the overall quality of the faculty? Is the nature of academic work such that the best we can do is use traditionally messy measures of quality—such as one's degree-granting institution or the status of one's mentor? Hilltop seemed to do this best by adhering closely to faculty procedures for saying no or yes to spouse and partner hires. What need to change are views that relegate spouses and partners to second-class status just because they are given assistance.

Such assistance was not criticized thirty years ago when many of today's senior faculty obtained their positions through personal contacts and the recommendations of their mentors (Caplow and McGee 1958; Burke 1988). Several of the department chairs we spoke with across the case study sites described situations where the spouse had turned out to be a better scholar than the initial hire. However, the question remains of how we can value such ascriptive characteristics as race and sex in searches yet not sacrifice the quality that is believed to emerge from open searches. One might ask also if we impose higher standards in a "search of one" than we do in an open search. After all, we often adjust our expectations when we see the vitae of candidates in a regular search. Unfortunately, our cases do not shed much light on this issue. Successful responses to the dual-career problem require addressing these questions.

Planning for the Unexpected

In a typical faculty search, it is not known in advance which candidate will eventually be offered a job, let alone whether this candidate has a spouse or partner seeking a faculty position. If the candidate does have a spouse or partner, that person's area of expertise will be unknown as well. Consequently, once the hiring unit decides to make an offer and learns that the candidate's spouse also seeks a position, the department chair must scurry around trying to arrange something. Neither the home of the original hire nor the department being asked to hire the spouse or partner has much time to plan for an unanticipated colleague. Such accommodations can create difficulties for institutions in terms of both short- and long-range planning.

Even when it seems desirable to accommodate spouses or partners, institutions must do so carefully. As an academic administrator at Heartland University explained: "You are going to damage the quality of your programs in two ways: you are going to distort the curriculum, especially in small departments. If you have a feel of the areas that need to be covered, the more you hire people that don't fit the program, [the more] you are doing some kind of damage to that program. Second, if you bend on quality and take somebody who is kind of good, without going through a national search, you may not be getting as good a person as you can."

As this quotation illustrates, policies or practices for hiring faculty spouses or partners present planning challenges for institutions and for their academic units. How do colleges and universities attempt to provide legitimate faculty opportunities for qualified spouses or partners when they have little prior knowledge of their existence or their disciplines yet not distort their academic programs? The unanticipated appearance of a faculty spouse or partner may create tensions between identified faculty needs and unplanned opportunities.

The bulk of our discussion of these challenges is directed toward tenured and tenure-track positions and addresses accommodation efforts at the department and college levels. Unlike hiring spouses or partners as temporary instructors or for non-tenure-track positions, hiring for tenured or tenure-track positions involves a major, long-term commitment. For this reason, dual-career policies or practices that seek to find or create tenure-track positions for spouses or partners face particular challenges in balancing plans for faculty needs with the ability to respond to such requests.

Our case studies have highlighted several approaches. At Belle State, for example, spouse and partner accommodation is handled completely ad hoc. There is no formal policy and therefore no specific pot of money set aside for the purpose. No institutional planning for such hires occurs—they are dealt with case by case. Likewise, little institutional planning is necessary when two faculty members share a position unless additional resources, such as benefits, are necessary. However, whenever resources are centrally committed for hiring spouses or partners into tenure-track faculty lines (or even into short-term, nontenure lines), some planning is necessary. Planning takes on added significance any time a tenure-track position is on the table. Heartland, Riverdale, and Hilltop each had committed some central pool of money for the express purpose of hiring spouses and partners. In the cases of Riverdale and Hilltop, funds are available for tenure-track lines; at Heartland the money is used to support short-term positions. Needless to say, some institutional planning is necessary to ensure that such resources are available.

Beyond the mere availability of funds, at Riverdale and Hilltop the Provost's Office played an additional role in deciding whether to cover one-third of the accompanying spouse or partner's salary. That is, in order for departments to take advantage of the institution-wide policy of allocating tenure-track positions for spouse and partner hires, the provost at each institution had to agree. However, these decisions did not seem to involve any formal human resources planning at the institutional level at either university. When we asked our contacts at Hilltop what criteria the provost used for deciding whether to contribute one-third of a salary, a department chair said, "[I assume he would ask,] Is this good for the college? Or is this good for the university? Do we have the money is obviously an important question. Does this fit the intent of the program? Or is it a legitimate use of the program [dual-career policy] even if it is not sort of narrowly within the restrictions of the program?" This chair was suggesting that the provost, in the absence of formal planning to account for spouse or partner hires, would use his larger sense of the needs of the entire university (informal planning) in determining whether he would contribute one-third of a salary. Of course, two units could make such a hire by covering the entire salary themselves.

Administrators at Riverdale describe a similar procedure for determining when to invoke the Bridge Program. A department chair at Riverdale said that all three units involved—the provost, the academic unit making the original hire, and the unit hiring the spouse or partner—would be very cautious in allocating limited resources.

Aside from making resources available and deciding how and when to use them, the tension between requests to accommodate and planning seems to be much more keenly felt at the academic unit level because of the way colleges create their budgets and manage limited resources. At research universities like Riverdale, Hilltop, and Heartland, money for faculty is usually decentralized and placed in academic department budgets that are overseen and "controlled" by the dean of the college. Therefore, planning for faculty needs and allocation of money to support faculty primarily take place at the department, school, or college level. Departments may have more control or less control over their own budgets, but one common practice is to assign faculty lines, or positions, to departments. These lines typically have their own budget codes, and each has the amount of the "occupant's" salary specified in the line. A department typically has a fixed number of lines, and it is usually difficult to get new permanent tenure-track lines because they must either come from the provost or result from reallocation of resources within a school or college. Universities and their schools and colleges differ in what happens to a line (and the money in that line) when a faculty member leaves. In some cases the money reverts to either a dean or a provost. In other cases the line stays with the department. Among our case study institutions there was some evidence that lines are increasingly reverting to either a dean or a provost for reallocation rather than remaining in departments. However, in the hearts and minds of faculty, the lines "belong" to departments. Lines vacated long ago are often still referred to by the names of their former occupants—"the Smith line" or "the Jones line."

The topic of lines and budgeting is important because they bear on the creation of effective approaches to dual-career accommodation. Because Riverdale, Hilltop, and Heartland all had limited resources, allocating a faculty line to a spouse or partner was often seen as particularly difficult decision. As one academic dean at Heartland University explained, "You have a spouse who is not in one of your priority areas, and then you try and get the deans to say that if we accept this person it is not going to lower the probability of getting that regular position we have been in line for [and presumably need]. And often those assurances are given; but when positions are really divvied out, it's hard not to think, 'well, we just gave somebody to that department.'" Thus, the worry is always whether the department will somehow be penalized by not getting the position it has planned for because it hired someone it hadn't planned on. The problem is exacerbated by the tendency of departments to feel ownership of and control over their lines.

Hilltop University takes a somewhat different approach to faculty lines and budgeting, talking about "pots of money" rather than faculty lines. Although one dean said people still think about lines with names attached, the "pot of money" concept has potential advantages from the perspective of accommodating spouses and partners. As an associate dean explained, "Well, now we collapse this line [vacated faculty position] and move the money into what we now call a tenure/tenure-track reserve. And it's money. It's got money in it. While technically there's an FTE associated with the reserve—somebody's at 3 1/2 FTE and x amount of money—the FTE is virtually irrelevant." Although some colleges at Hilltop took a different approach, the university as a whole was trying to move away from the named-line approach to the "pots of money" approach. This approach would seemingly make it easier for a department to contribute one-third of a spouse or partner salary because symbolically, there is quite a difference between giving up $15,000 (one-third of a salary) and losing a line. Of course, there is still the problem of having sufficient money in the "pot" to search for and hire the next planned faculty member. Yet the pot of money approach seems quite flexible.

Riverdale's Bridge Program requires departmental planning, especially by the department employing the accompanying spouse. The Bridge Program, as the associate provost explained, "is only for tenure-track money. . . . What they are doing is that they are aware that they are going to have a retirement in two or three years down the road . . . They have to show there will be an opening. They need to know because the Bridge Program only works in terms of the permanent appointment." The Bridge Program will provide financial support for three years, but at the end of the three years it is assumed that the receiving department will have a tenure-track position available for the spouse or partner. Because at this point the employing department will have to finance the entire position, it is inclined to do so only to fulfill real needs. As the associate provost explained, "This whole Bridge Program is about mortgaging your future. If somebody really wants to do something and all they can do at the moment is 20 percent but they can show over the progression of years how this is going to happen [become fully funded], we certainly won't say 'I'm sorry.' That absolutely defeats the whole notion of the program." Therefore the Bridge Program requires academic units to plan their faculty needs far in advance and, in the case of spouse or partner hire, to think seriously about whether they want to devote a future full-time position to that person. Although the Bridge Program allows departments to act spontaneously, it does force a department to think carefully about its future needs.

This kind of planning may be particularly difficult for small departments with fewer positions to begin with, in departments frequently called on to hire spouses or partners, and for more resource-starved universities. Although all three universities in our study complained about limited resources, they understood this term differently. In a resource-scarce environment like this, the costs of "giving up a line" may be greater because the chances of getting the line for an originally intended position may be less. Administrators at Heartland agreed that making too many spouse or partner hires distorts or contradicts efforts to rank faculty staffing needs; however, they rarely hired spouses for tenure-track positions. At the time of our visit they were evaluating their program and policy and thus had thought at length about how to combine the various hiring priorities facing universities. As the dean of the College of Liberal Arts and Sciences at Heartland said:

> I am sensitive to the priority issue, and I am sensitive to affirmative action issues, diversity hiring, and that sort of thing, so I would like to find a way to serve all the needs we just talked about. One way to do that, to honor all of these objectives, is for the institution as a whole to identify a set of positions as we authorize searches and hold some positions vacant that we are not searching on. Then, when we have couples come along that fit into that broader range of institutionally prioritized positions . . . rather than just looking for one person in arts and sciences, we look at couples who might fit into a total of 300 positions that fit into our plan for the next five years. We are always looking a little more broadly than just our hiring for this year. We look at hiring priorities on a five-year horizon for the whole institution, which would allow us to look for couples.

Most administrators at Heartland acknowledged having discussed this plan without ever acting on it. Some talked about the need to expand the planning to include all positions at neighboring smaller colleges as well. Another department chair suggested guidelines that would help new chairs decide when to take advantage of the Faculty Fellows Program:

> I would put together a simple scheme dividing it into certain criteria, that is, the person's area, and there needs to be a sliding scale from this is exactly the kind of person we would want to hire to this would duplicate two people we already have. If you absolutely insist on the top, exactly what you want on your list, then this is not going to work. If you get too careless, you are going to destroy quality. There needs to be some sort of sliding scale. I would begin with "really want" and scale down to "could use" and trail off to "wouldn't really fit our program at all."

Long-range planning will almost surely help to ensure that spouse and partner hires do not distort the curriculum and research missions of departments and colleges. However, a long range plan that is too tightly defined could interfere with hiring an accompanying spouse or partner because it might not allow for serendipitous hires. Long-range planning is further complicated by the impossibility of anticipating the academic specialty of an accompanying spouse or partner who might appear unexpectedly. As one administrator at Hilltop cautioned:

> Here's another practical rule of thumb. I try not to mortgage the future too far, but I don't like to stop short of pursuing something because of the long term. I think long term but try not to think of all of these things that will be problems down the line . . . You could torpedo any deal if you get too locked into that long-term futuristic, very hypothetical, speculative thinking. What I try to do is to focus on something we really want to do. The long-term consequences are somewhat nebulous, but we know that the immediate consequences are very favorable. It may be a mistake, but I try to err in the direction of trying to move forward.

This attitude reflects the views of a relatively resource-rich, top-notch research university that is always looking to capitalize on its strengths. A more cautious, resource-strapped university may think differently. There is no one-size-fits-all formula for planning in general, let alone planning that includes spouse or partner accommodation. Needs, resources, and value commitments, among other factors, must be considered case by case to ensure that planning best reflects the particularities of each institution.

The Intersection of Dual-Career Hiring and Faculty Autonomy

One of the concerns expressed by opponents of dual-career accommodation is that it diminishes faculty autonomy in hiring. The perception is that dual-career accommodation is an administrative initiative that interferes with the faculty's right to choose their colleagues. What may not be commonly recognized, however, is that it is usually the faculty in the department making the initial hire who want another group of faculty to agree to hire the person's spouse or partner. The administrator, in most cases, merely serves as a middleman or broker. Regardless whether the request to hire a spouse or partner is from another group of faculty or from an administrator, faculty are concerned that their right to have a say in the hiring of their colleagues is being trampled.

This "right" is elaborated in the 1966 Joint Statement of Government of Colleges and Universities by the American Association of University Professors, American Council on Education, and Association of Governing Boards of Universities and Colleges. The statement reads:

Faculty status and related matters are primarily a faculty responsibility. This area includes appointments, reappointments, decisions not to reappoint, promotions, the granting of tenure, and dismissal. The primary responsibility of the faculty for such matters is based upon the fact that its judgment is central to general educational policy. Furthermore, scholars in the particular field or activity have the chief competence for judging the work of their colleagues.

Despite the increasing presence of professional administrators in higher education and the erosion of shared governance, faculty still desire, and in most cases have, considerable autonomy in hiring decisions (Finkelstein 1984).

Recognition of the faculty's right to control hiring helps to explain why all the case study respondents were quick to point out that no accommodation is made without the approval of the department faculty. Repeatedly, administrators and faculty alike stated, "We would never foist someone upon a department by administrative fiat. The departments receiving the accompanying spouses have to want them as colleagues." That is also why all accommodations, whether they entailed placing an accompanying spouse or partner in a tenure-track position or a more temporary job, involved the departmental faculty in the decision making.

While department faculty at all our case study sites had a say in hiring accompanying spouses or partners, the external perception of such hires is that the procedure circumvents faculty authority in favor of administrative priorities. As described in the previous section, this problem is exacerbated by the system institutions use to grant faculty lines. As faculty lines grow scarcer, concern about who is making hiring decisions intensifies. Further, deciding whether to hire an accompanying spouse or partner is fraught with political considerations beyond the hire itself. Departments may be hesitant to turn down a resource offered from above. After all, being granted a faculty position in the current economic situation is generally considered a boon. Further, rejecting a potential hire may make a department appear uncooperative and therefore less deserving of resources in the future. At the same time, departments do not want to take every hire that is offered to them for fear of becoming (or being perceived as) dumping grounds for the spouses and partners of faculty members in other disciplines. And departments may fear that when they hire an accompanying spouse or partner, they will be less likely in the future to receive permission to fill a position they really want to fill. Department faculty may feel damned if they do, damned if they don't.

Either way, many believe that even when faculty do have a say in hiring, the political nature of the situation does not allow them to make a decision as they might in a "regular" search. Thus the concern remains about how much dual-career hiring policies affect faculty autonomy.

Concluding Comment

There are no clear-cut solutions to most of the problems discussed in this chapter. "Fairness," "faculty quality," and "autonomy" are normative concepts that are open to philosophical discussion and debate. Different institutions will no doubt have different understandings of these concepts and how to address them. The growing number of dual-career academic couples calls on faculty and administrators to think seriously about how these key principles ought to be conceptualized. It may be concluded that the prevailing understandings of these concepts are entirely adequate and that institutions ought to conform their practices to them. It may just as well turn out that, given demographic and other social changes, the dominant understanding will seem dated and unhelpful. If the latter is the case, practices regarding dual-career hiring ought to be brought into line with new, refined understandings of fairness, quality, autonomy, and related concepts.

Questions about the legal requirements for accommodating married and partnered faculty and the implications of spouse and partner hiring for a unit's overall personnel needs are more "practical" in nature. Institutions can make sure that their dual-career policies are consistent with existing laws, rules, and regulations and ensure that their accommodation practices take into account current and future personnel and institutional needs. There is no recipe that all institutions can follow to arrive at the "right" answer. But once the more basic conceptual questions are ironed out, planning is a practical matter to be undertaken in light of the specific missions, constraints, and resources—the whole complex of attributes—that largely constitute any individual college or university.

10 | The Two-Body Problem Revisited

Conclusions and Recommendations

In this chapter we revisit the reasons colleges and universities ought to be concerned with the needs of dual-career academic couples. We begin by discussing some shifting assumptions about the role that institutions of higher education play in managing human resources and caring for the quality of life. Then we present some overarching conclusions drawn from our research and suggest some questions that institutions both with and without policies ought to consider. Finally, we discuss some key conclusions and recommendations for each type of accommodation discussed in chapters 4 through 8.

Shifting Assumptions

Academia, as an employer, has had a history of being less concerned than the business world with providing resources to recruit, develop, and retain its employees. This is remarkable given that in awarding tenure a college or university is potentially making a lifetime commitment to faculty. In particular, concerns about the quality of life outside the work environment, such as the employment of spouses or partners, day care, and other family concerns, have until recently largely been ignored by those in academe. There are several explanations for this. In her study of the academic labor market at research universities, Burke (1988) suggests that higher education has operated under the assumption that a faculty position is so desirable that the institution need do nothing to make it more attractive. Consequently there is little incentive to care about improving work life. Second, the existence of an academic labor market where far too many qualified candidates compete for any single position also allows academic institutions to ignore quality of life. A third explanation is that the normative structures of university life are based on a model of self-reliance in which academics who need assistance of any kind are considered weak and are to be weeded out through the selection and promotion process. These structures define an ideal academic worker as one who is, in essence, married to his work, leaving little time for a personal life (Williams 1999). Further, the professoriat presumes a singularity of purpose that precludes worrying about the needs of one's partner, let alone other family concerns. In this regard, some have described the professoriat as being "built upon men's normative paths and assum[ing] freedom from competing responsibilities, such as family, that generally affect women more than men. In such a system, [academics] with families are cumulatively disadvantaged" (Grant, Kennelly, and Ward 2000, 66). Under these norms, the institution bears less responsibility than the individual for success within the system. Those who experience difficulties leave the profession, to be replaced from among the many who want to be professors.

Today, however, colleges and universities are beginning to recognize the institutional benefits of acknowledging and responding to the personal and professional concerns of their employees. Burke (1988) noted that the change toward a human resources perspective is a result of intensified competition for top graduates among research universities and between higher education and industry. Changes in the demography of those earning doctorates are also a factor forcing institutions to accommodate the needs of their faculty. Specifically, there are more women entering the academic profession, and many of them are married to other academics. And younger male faculty members are more likely than ever before to be part of a dual-career couple (Astin and Milem 1997). Colleges and universities no longer have the luxury of assuming that faculty members are unencumbered by external concerns, since life outside work is taking on increased importance for workers in all fields. Further, administrators are slowly coming to take seriously the research demonstrating that job satisfaction, institutional loyalty, and retention depend on the supportiveness of the work environment (Bond, Galinsky, and Swanberg 1998).

As one piece of evidence that academic institutions are making the shift toward family friendliness, the American Association of University Professors recently issued several recommendations, including providing extra time on the tenure clock for bearing and caring for children, coordinating the university's academic calendar with that of local school districts, and providing onsite child care. While not directly related to dual-career hiring, these initiatives certainly demonstrate that those in academe are aware that personal and professional concerns overlap and that academic institutions have something to gain by helping their employees succeed in both realms. The creation of the College and University Work/Family Association (CUWFA), whose mission is to provide information on work/family issues within the specialized environment of higher education, is further evidence of this trend. CUWFA offers services to support the diverse group of professionals contributing to the development of work/family programs and policies on campus: human resource administrators, student services administrators, work/family managers, child care and elder care program directors, senior administrators, faculty, and others. The founding of CUWFA is part of a larger trend in the creation of work-life centers on college and university campuses. Such centers are a popular means for college campuses to help faculty, staff, and students balance their work, study, personal, and family lives. The services such centers offer vary, but they may include on-site child care, emergency and backup child care assistance, child care subsidies, parent education and consultation, elder care programs, and workshop series designed to help workers learn how to balance their personal and professional lives. Work-life centers provide another example of higher education's recognition that the old way of doing business—the self-reliant approach—is no longer going to work, especially if institutions want to recruit the best faculty, encourage productivity, and keep loyal employees.

Overarching Conclusions

Recognition of the Importance of Dual-Career Accommodation

Our research supports the contention that colleges and universities are beginning to recognize the extraprofessional needs of dual-career couples and are willing to try to help them, whether through a formal policy or ad hoc. All the institutions we visited, and most of those we surveyed, recognized that family-friendly policies pay off in faculty productivity and satisfaction. That said, many of the resolutions of dual-career accommodation requests, even at places with formal policies, rely on serendipity, timing, and flexibility. Clearly, an accommodation is not going to be made every time there is a request, nor will spouses or partners of faculty members necessarily get the jobs they want. Nevertheless, an academic institution expresses goodwill when it tries to help a couple find work—this goodwill is likely to increase its chances of hiring the desired candidate and may secure the couple's loyalty.

Failure to Make All Couples Happy

Despite the goodwill expressed by having a dual-career accommodation policy, no single policy or approach is going to yield results that satisfy everyone. This is especially true given that most colleges and universities recognize that short-term appointments are easier, more flexible, and therefore
more common than accommodations involving tenure-track positions. Let
us illustrate with an example from one of our case study sites. Joan and Sam
are married; both have doctorates in English, and both were on the job market at the same time. Sam applied for the position at Belle State because Joan
was a candidate for a position at a nearby university. In fact, Sam was offered
a tenure-track position at Belle State while Joan was offered a three-year appointment at the other university. Because the other university was a three-
hour drive away, Joan rented an apartment in the town near where she was
employed and commuted once a week. Subsequently a tenure-track position
opened at Belle State and Joan applied. She did not get the job, but she was
offered a lectureship that was not tenure track. Joan turned down that position and applied for and received a job as an academic adviser at Belle State.
Although Joan likes the advising job, she noted that "it . . . will make it
harder to get a regular teaching position, which is what I really want—a regular tenure-track position. Now, I'm not doing very much research because I
don't have time. I could teach a course, but it would be an overload." Joan en-
joys working with students, and the job pays almost as much as a faculty position. As she says, "It's a good job in a lot of ways. It's just not a teaching
job." From Sam and Joan's perspective, the institution didn't do enough to
help her get a tenure-track position, which was her ultimate goal.

Sam and Joan's situation raises several issues that dual-career couples are
forced to face. Joan clearly thought of herself as being qualified for the tenure-track position that opened at Belle State. She was not interested in the
more temporary position that was offered to her. She explained, "I could
have taken what, to me, was an unacceptable position, which was a lectureship, teaching an extremely heavy load in composition. This was more or
less a GTA position, and I'm already an experienced professor." So she had
to face the thought of staying around Belle State after being rejected for a
tenure-track position, accepting what she saw as a graduate teaching assistant's position, or finding an alternative—the advising position. Furthermore, Sam had to come to terms with the fact that the university didn't want

him badly enough to make a better accommodation for Joan. In Joan's words, "They were apparently willing to let Sam go." From Sam and Joan's perspective, Belle State didn't do enough to help them. However, the administrators and faculty involved felt they had done all they could to accommodate the couple. The department chair did find the funds to hire Joan for the adjunct position, even though the department faculty had not thought she was the best candidate for the tenure-track position. The institution believed it had done what it could to support both Sam and Joan, even though the couple interpreted the assistance more negatively. Conflicting perceptions like these are commonplace in dual-career hiring situations.

Desirability of the Initial Hire

Based on our analysis, it is clear that dual-career accommodations are most likely where the initial hires are highly desired—whether because of their national stature, their research interests, their backgrounds, or some other unique characteristic they bring to the institution. Clearly, when a university is recruiting a star, it is more willing to make an accommodation when hiring at a lower rank who has yet to make a name. In terms of diversity, there appears to be some discrepancy between word and deed. According to our survey of provosts, one of the stated goals for a dual-career hiring policy is recruiting a faculty that is diverse in both race and gender. Our case study research, however, is inconclusive concerning how well these goals are achieved. Certainly hiring a heterosexual dual-career couple would bring in both a male and female faculty member. Although such hires increase the number of women on the faculty, they do not increase the percentage of women. Further, at our case study sites, the vast majority of dual-career accommodations were made for whites rather than for racial or ethnic minorities. Our findings were somewhat at odds with those of others who have concluded that dual-career policies help recruit minority faculty members (Astin and Milem 1997; Loeb 1997; Perkins 1997; Smith et al. 1996). For example, Loeb (1997) found that as a result of its dual-career policy, the University of Illinois at Urbana-Champaign improved its recruitment of minority faculty. Indeed, because some research has demonstrated that minorities with doctorates are more likely to be members of dual-career academic couples than are whites, these policies have the potential to help diversify the faculty (Astin and Milem 1997; Perkins 1997; Smith et al. 1996).

Minimizing Problems

An important characteristic of institutions with successful dual-career policies is that they have minimized the problems and instead focused on the
possibilities. As discussed in chapter 9 and evinced by a recent article in the
Chronicle of Higher Education titled "The Backlash against Hiring Couples"
(Wilson 2001), five aspects of dual-career accommodation are of particular
concern: fairness, legality, quality, the tension between departmental needs
and spouse and partner hires, and faculty autonomy in the hiring process.

Fairness as a Concern, Fairness as a Solution

To recap briefly, there is some concern over the fairness of dual-career accommodation policies. For the past half century, institutions of higher education have tried to eliminate discrimination in hiring and other practices.
It is widely agreed that race, gender, and ethnicity, among other characteristics, should not factor into colleges' and universities' hiring decisions except in a positive manner. At question is whether marital or partner status
should be an exception to this general rule. Should couples be given special
consideration? Will doing so discriminate against applicants who happen to
be single? Different types of accommodation approaches—for example, a
relocation assistance program that is open to all new hires—do mitigate un-
easiness about offering spouses or partners of sought-after hires an advantage not available to everyone. Institutions that have successful dual-career
policies believe they are fair and often deal with questions about fairness by
carrying out the policy openly and evenly. Further, they recognize that the realities of those applying for academic positions (more women and more
dual-career couples) may require new formulations of what it means to be
fair. We are not suggesting that concerns about fairness are not legitimate,
but we do think the issue is not as black and white as some would have us believe. Obviously it is up to individual institutions to reconcile the fairness of
their approach to dual-career accommodations and to act accordingly.

Legality as a Concern, Legality as a Solution

Second, there are questions (and myths) about the legality of dual-career hiring. Is dual-career accommodation a form of nepotism? Does such accommodation jibe with affirmative action guidelines and regulations? Variations
in state law and institutional policies affect the answers to these questions.
That said, we and other scholars who have studied this issue (Shoben 1997)

have found no explicit legal challenges to dual-career accommodation policies. As long as a policy does not on its face or in practice discriminate against individuals based on gender, race, ethnicity, disability, age, religion, or veterans' status, it appears that it is legal. Administrators would be wise to consult the university's attorney as well as the Equal Opportunity Office to ensure that their policy is in line with all relevant statutes.

Quality as a Concern, Quality as a Solution

The third concern about dual-career accommodations has to do with faculty quality. It is widely believed, rightly or wrongly, that when accommodations are made, one member of the accommodated couple will likely be less qualified than his or her spouse or partner. Of concern is whether a person is hired based on merit or based on marital or partner status. Also of concern is whether the accompanying spouse or partner is less qualified than other possible candidates in a traditional search. This concern is obviously greater when a tenure-track position is created for an accompanying spouse or partner than with some other form of accommodation. Institutions with dual-career policies are clear that the only way to make hiring the accompanying spouse or partner viable from an institutional standpoint is to make sure that those doing the hiring pay careful attention to quality. Such policies make explicit the necessity of reviewing the experience and backgrounds of all potential hires introduced through a dual-career policy and having the faculty and administrators involved vote on whether the candidate meets the criteria necessary for the position. Failing to do this could indeed compromise quality.

Future Needs as a Concern, Long-Range Planning as a Solution

Fourth, institutions must consider the effect that hiring an accompanying spouse or partner may have on present and future personnel needs. Spouses and partners of academics are not randomly distributed across disciplines, and it is likely that some departments may be asked more frequently to accommodate them. Failing to consider the present and future needs of the department, as well as of the institution more broadly, may affect the fundamental character of the department and its programs. It is essential that departments, schools, and the university as a whole pay attention to their future faculty needs when they consider hiring an accompanying spouse or partner into a faculty position. This may require that academic units anticipate future needs.

Faculty Autonomy as a Concern, Faculty Autonomy as a Solution

Last, there is the concern that accommodating dual-career couples will compromise faculty control over hiring. Here the concerns over faculty quality and autonomy merge. It is widely believed that faculty, in contrast to administrators or some other party, are best able to judge the merits of prospective colleagues. Hence, control over hiring legitimately belongs to faculty. As we explained in the section on quality, dual-career accommodation policies ought to give the department faculty involved in hiring accompanying spouses or partners a say in whether to make the hire. Hiring faculty colleagues continues to be a crucial part of faculty governance that ought to be continued, especially in the wake of policies that involve hiring individuals through other than regular means.

Summary of Concerns and Solutions

Concerns about fairness, legality, quality, balancing needs, and faculty autonomy are legitimate, but they are also more complicated than some on the different sides of the issue would have us believe. Administrators and faculty members at the institutions we visited recognized these concerns and the potential problems but were able to reconcile them with what they saw as positive solutions. Clearly dual-career couples present a difficult situation for academic institutions, and no single answer is appropriate for every college and university. Rather, institutions ought to consider their culture, size, resources, location, and other specific characteristics in order to determine what is most appropriate. There are two other matters to be taken into account as institutions consider developing and implementing dual-career policies: first, the unique concerns faced by smaller colleges; second, whether a policy ought to include both spouses and unmarried partners.

The Unique Situation Faced by Small Colleges

Because of their size and limited resources, we recognize that small colleges have less freedom to employ the accompanying spouse or partner than larger institutions might have. As such, when deans of small colleges were asked to provide advice for others attempting to respond to the needs of dual-career couples, one of the clear responses was that their communities were too small and too close-knit to promise potential faculty members that something would eventually open up for their partners and spouses. As one dean stated, "Never promise something you can't deliver just to recruit someone. If you fail to deliver, you will have made someone very unhappy and bitter, and this is too small a place to have that happen." As a result of this caveat, administrators at small colleges were very hesitant to promise any form of assistance—although they might go so far as to say, "We will try." Deans at small colleges also said that accommodations, if they occur, would be ad hoc, not the result of a formal policy.

Limitations due to constrained resources and small faculty numbers, however, do not mean that smaller institutions should neglect the needs of dual-career couples. Considering the merits of allowing faculty to share or split positions or engaging in joint advertising with nearby institutions, for example, does offer small colleges a means of assisting dual-career couples.

Accommodating both Married and Unmarried Partners

Throughout this text we have purposely used the term "spouses and partners" in describing dual-career accommodation policies. We used this terminology in our survey, in part because we were unsure whether colleges and universities that had dual-career policies limited their assistance to married couples or used it more liberally to include unmarried partners. What we learned from our survey is that slightly more than half (55 percent) of those with such policies extend them to both married and unmarried partners. At most of our case study sites, we also found that unmarried partners were tacitly included in the policies as a group that the institution was willing to assist if asked. We found, however, that institutions with dual-career accommodation policies did not call attention to whether their policy was open to unmarried partners. We realized that this quietness was purposeful and was meant to avoid criticism from those who might oppose including unmarried partners and those who might insist that they be included. While our opinion is that dual-career accommodation policies ought to be open to both spouses and partners, the ultimate decision rests with the administrators and faculty members at each institution.

Questions to Ask When Developing a Dual-Career Policy

For institutions of all sizes that do not yet have a dual-career policy, it is important to consider a number of factors when deciding whether to create such a policy and, if so, what kind. Because each college and university is unique, addressing these questions is the best advice we can offer institutions as they plan how best to respond to the needs of current and aspiring academics in dual-career partnerships.

- How well is the institution meeting its faculty recruitment goals?
- How does the institution's current approach to dual-career hiring advance or inhibit attainment of recruitment goals?
- What type of person is the institution trying to recruit? Approaches for recruiting new assistant professors might differ radically from those used for more senior scholars.
- What opportunities for professional employment exist nearby or within the institution, and is the institution currently availing itself of these opportunities?
- What range of assistance that might be offered—from creating a tenure-track position to using off-campus networks to place an accompanying spouse or partner—is the institution willing to consider?
- How will the institution weigh the needs of individual faculty members against the needs of the institution as a whole? That is, how will it balance the serendipitous nature of the opportunity offered by dual-career hires with overall curricular and hiring needs?
- How will affirmative action at the institution be affected by a dual-career policy?
- Finally, what barriers and opportunities are unique to the institution and its culture in deciding whether and how to assist dual-career couples?

Questions for Institutions That Have a Dual-Career Policy

For institutions that currently have a policy, our research offers some suggestions about factors to consider when assessing whether it is meeting their goals and needs.

- Are all deans, department chairs, and faculty on hiring committees aware of the policy?
- To what extent does the policy reinforce institutional values or definitions of faculty quality?
- Are the policies being implemented in a way that is consistent with federal and state laws and other institutional policies?
- Are faculty members worried or upset about the effect of the policy on faculty autonomy or faculty quality?

- How important is the policy in recruiting and retaining faculty?
- What contributions do the accommodated spouses and partners make to the institution?

In our exploration we found that too few institutions that have such policies have assessed their effectiveness. Furthermore, many have not attempted to answer these questions. Exploring the effects of one's dual-career accommodation policy would help those implementing it to make necessary improvements. An assessment can also help respond to the naysayers who believe such policies erode the institution's quality.

Conclusions and Recommendations by Type of Assistance

As we have described them in this book, there are six broad approaches currently being used to help spouses and partners of academics find suitable employment. The college or university can create a relocation office or use on-campus facilities to help an accompanying spouse or partner find work in the region, as well as help the couple adjust to their new community. Second, it can hire an accompanying spouse or partner in an administrative position. Third, an institution may develop either a formal or an ad hoc policy to hire the accompanying spouse or partner for a part-time, adjunct, or non tenure-track faculty position. Fourth, an institution may create a shared position in which the initial hire and his or her spouse or partner share a single academic line. Another option is to use existing relationships with nearby institutions and advertise positions jointly. Sixth, in relatively rare situations, the institution may create a tenure-track position for a spouse or partner. This last approach is most likely at large research universities. Specific conclusions and recommendations based on each of these approaches are reviewed below.

Relocation Assistance

We can offer numerous reasons why most institutions ought to provide relocation assistance to prospective and new employees and their spouses and partners, and we know of no arguments against doing so. Although this is a more difficult undertaking for small colleges, large universities definitely should offer such services. Indeed, the goodwill created, we believe, far outweighs the cost. Candidates appreciate having an office dedicated to helping them make the transition to a new community. Such a service can be made available to every new hire, whether the person has a spouse or partner or is single, thus mitigating claims of unfairness. Relocation assistance offices also can encourage cooperation between academic institutions and the local community. The comprehensiveness of services offered by such an office may vary greatly, from providing information to all job candidates about the local community (real estate, education, community services) to offering career counseling and placement assistance to spouses or partners of newly hired university employees. Some offices even offer reciprocal services to employees of businesses in the community. For institutions that choose to offer such a service, below are some more specific recommendations.

- Establish a relocation office and appoint a coordinator. Especially at institutions that hire a large number of new employees each year, the workload would be too great for one existing staff member to take on as an additional task. Smaller institutions may be able to use existing services such as a human resources employee or someone from the student career services center to offer similar assistance to newly hired professional staff.
- Provide financial support. Such support is necessary if institutions want to provide comprehensive relocation services. Costs include phones, faxes, postage, printing a brochure, and hiring a coordinator. There are less expensive ways to provide such services, though the assistance will be less comprehensive. For example, an institution can consider allowing the spouses or partners of new hires to use the career placement services for students or get assistance from the human resources department. Contracting out these services to a local agency, if one exists, is another option.
- Produce a brochure to publicize the scope of services offered and eligibility for them. A program brochure and Web site are useful tools for summarizing and promoting services offered. The brochure should be disseminated to all those who are conducting searches so that candidates are made aware of such services before or during an on-campus interview. This document should stress that the institution will help spouses and partners find employment but that the institution is not responsible for finding them jobs. Institutions should make sure they have the means of helping in the ways they claim to help. In other words, don't promise more than you can deliver.
- The brochure and other related information should be given to all deans, department chairs, and search committee chairs and made available to

prospective candidates depending on the relocation office's policy (e.g., all candidates, all finalists, or only persons offered a position).

- The relocation office should serve as a clearinghouse for on-campus as well as off-campus positions and should assist the accompanying spouse or partner with making on-campus contacts. The relocation specialist is in an ideal position to help an accompanying spouse or partner find some sort of administrative position at the institution. As with other services offered, no promises ought to be made regarding on-campus employment.
- Relocation offices should participate in career networks with nearby academic institutions and with business and industry. The most successful of these networks have a coordinator who is in regular communication with community groups as well as business, industry, and other organizations offering employment.
- Persons working in relocation services may wish to address some of the emotional aspects of relocation. At the least, they must decide whether and to what extent they will do personal counseling. Relocation can be very stressful, particularly for an accompanying spouse or partner, and as our case studies illustrate, this stress can affect the work of the relocation specialist. In addition to providing information about employment options, relocation offices can also be of great assistance with logistics— helping the family find a place to live, learn where to shop, find a church, and so on.
- To ensure continued support of relocation services, it is important to document past successes. The relocation specialist should keep careful account of the numbers of clients placed and the kinds of jobs found and whatever additional information is relevant to an institution's particular situation.

On-Campus Administrative Positions

Although we did not devote a chapter to the topic of hiring accompanying spouses or partners into on-campus administrative positions, we believe it is a viable solution for many dual-career academic couples and the institutions they work for. However, we could not find a case study site that had created a regular procedure for accommodating dual-career couples in this manner. That said, we learned from our survey of provosts that many institutions do make such accommodations ad hoc. Indeed, for larger institutions, hiring an accompanying spouse or partner into an administrative position is one of the more common types of accommodation. Depending on the background and interests of the spouse or partner and the needs of the institution, there are a host of employment possibilities, especially at larger institutions. If the spouse or partner has an advanced degree, for example, he or she may be uniquely suited to work as an academic adviser, a service learning or learning community coordinator, an administrator for an honors or international program, or any number of other student services positions. Indeed, hiring someone with academic credentials is directly in line with current trends that call for greater cooperation and communication between student services and the academic community. If the accompanying spouse or partner is more interested in research, there may also be opportunities for those with academic credentials to work on soft-money research or training projects.

Opportunities are also typically available on campus for accompanying spouses or partners who do not have advanced degrees. Again, success at finding on-campus work for them will depend on their background and interests.

We contend that a relocation specialist would be in an ideal position to help an accompanying spouse or partner find suitable on-campus employment. These suggestions may be useful.

- The relocation specialist can help spouses and partners make the appropriate connections by informing them about position availability and by guiding them through the bureaucracy.
- If these relocation services are not available, we suggest that department chairs and deans become familiar with identifying available on-campus opportunities.

Short-Term Academic Positions

Short-term, non-tenure-track positions can take many forms. There are cases in which supposedly short-term appointments are renewed year after year, while in other cases the term "limited" is used literally. In some instances such positions are converted into regular tenure-track jobs, but in most cases, even when faculty contracts are repeatedly renewed, the basic conditions of employment never change. These positions remain non-tenure-track, typically with lower pay and higher teaching loads than tenure-track positions. In some cases faculty beginning in short-term appointments have the inside track when tenure-track jobs open and are successful in their bid for these jobs. In other instances having worked in a short-term position carries no advantage. There are practically no limits to the ways length of term, assignment of duties, requirements for reappointment, and other conditions of employment can be arrayed.

Given the wide variety of short-term, non-tenure-track arrangements, it should not be surprising that one of the most frequently encountered problems—for institutions and faculty alike—is unmet expectations. Being aware that some part-timers eventually gain full-time work, if not tenure-track positions, spouses or partners will often accept a limited-term appointment expecting that they too will end up with something more permanent. When this does not occur, the all but inevitable result is disappointment and frustration. While this is an extreme example, it is common for adjunct faculty to hold out hope that their position will improve; this hope is often unrealized. If hiring institutions do nothing more, they must communicate as clearly as possible what faculty in limited-term appointments may reasonably expect. Above all, they should not intimate that such a position will evolve into something more secure and long term unless this is a real possibility.

But can institutions do more than communicate the limitations of short-term appointments? Along with McNeil and Sher (1998), we believe they can. Below are a few suggestions.

- Colleges and universities might consider longer-term appointments. McNeil and Sher argue that longer-term appointments help morale by providing some sense of direction and stability. A three-year appointment, for example, lets a couple judge how well the tenure-track partner is progressing toward tenure and promotion, and this in turn enables them to plan for the next few years. Among the most stressful appointments are those reviewed every year. Given the academic calendar and the length of most review processes, a faculty member with a one-year contract has in reality only about six months' worth of relative security. There is no magic formula for determining the ideal short-term arrangement, but generally speaking couples—and arguably institutions—will be better served by appointments that are long enough for the couple to develop their career plans and to give the person in the short-term position some level of job security.
- Institutions should recognize the accomplishments of faculty in non-tenure-track appointments. Such recognition can boost morale. Adjunct fac-

ulty often invest significant time and energy in their work, in some cases rivaling that of their tenure-track colleagues. Why not recognize this hard work and its contribution to an institution's mission? Recognizing faculty achievements—even if this includes a monetary award—is inexpensive and may be regarded as a good investment when it increases productivity—a by-product often attributed to good faculty morale.

- Institutions can provide access to at least some institutional resources. This will alleviate the sense of marginalization commonly experienced by adjunct faculty. Funds for such things as scholarly travel, equipment, and supplies are basic to successful academic work. It is widely recognized that salary often falls considerably short of the effort part-timers expend. Shouldn't colleges and universities do all they can to better compensate their efforts? It is also common knowledge that time spent in adjunct positions generally detracts from faculty members' marketability. In light of adjuncts' contributions to an institution, shouldn't there be a sense of institutional responsibility to mitigate the worst effects of serving in these short-term appointments? A relatively modest investment in resources not only would help adjunct faculty in their own right but also, in all likelihood, would help the institution as well.

- Institutions can offer career assistance to faculty whose short-term appointments have terminated. Career counseling and help with résumé writing are two modest means of assistance. Only slightly more ambitious is helping them get funding for reentering the postdoctoral market—funding that in some disciplines exists on a small scale through federal agencies.

- Colleges and universities should evaluate their climate in terms of its friendliness toward non-tenure-track employees. As colleges and universities rely more and more heavily on adjunct faculty—regardless of whether these faculty are part of dual-career couples—it is essential to overall effectiveness to pay attention to part-time or even full-time non-tenure-track faculty. In many cases they carry heavy teaching loads in the institutions' core courses. We suspect tenure-track faculty might oppose such measures because they fear the trend away from tenure-track positions toward more temporary jobs. However, creating a positive culture for non-tenure-track faculty offers an opportunity to enhance the overall climate and learning environment on campus.

- Institutions must think carefully about the terms attached to people and positions. As we discussed in chapter 1, and as was illustrated in the case of Wildwood College (chapter 6), even the language used to refer to those with different kinds of appointments shapes how faculty are perceived, and how they perceive themselves. Terms such as "leading" and "trailing," for example, communicate the notion that one partner is more valuable than the other. Likewise with many of the terms used to differentiate between tenure-track and non-tenure-track faculty, especially when the latter are prefaced with a demeaning adverb, as in "She's just an adjunct." Attention to such concerns makes the academic climate that much more inviting and welcoming. Non-tenure-track appointments are a reality in academic life that is not going to go away—by some estimates, the majority of all new faculty hires are in some form of non-tenure-track position (Finkelstein, Seal, and Schuster 1998). Therefore institutions of higher education ought to work to improve the lives and working conditions of these academics rather than continuing to treat them as second-class citizens. Paying attention to them will benefit everyone at the institution.

Joint, Split, and Shared Positions

Whether they are called joint, split, or shared, positions in which two individuals share a single line offer important benefits to institutions and academic couples alike. Institutions have the benefit of two faculty members who are often more productive in their shared position than a single faculty member. Faculty couples have the benefit of working at the same institution and are generally better able to balance their work and home lives than if they were separated. Of course this arrangement also has costs, both for the college or university and for the academic couple. Typically, their salary and benefits will be at least somewhat higher than for a single faculty member. Office space, equipment, travel money, and other resources will normally exceed those needed by just one person. In all likelihood, however, while the institution will not get two faculty members for the price of one, it will get more (by almost any measure) than a single faculty member could provide. We currently do not know whether there is a point at which a college has too many individuals in shared positions, nor do we know what effects such positions have on institutional climate. Institutions that consider this option would be wise to monitor the number of such appointments and conduct an assessment to determine the effect on the academic community.

There are costs to faculty, too. Most obvious is lower pay. Even though faculty in shared positions can often supplement their one-half salary by extra teaching and other duties, they will not achieve the equivalent of a regular whole salary. This loss of income is offset not monetarily, but with greater freedom and flexibility. Our research suggests several factors that need to be taken into account by colleges and universities considering position sharing as a means of accommodation.

- It is important to recognize that position sharing can take many forms. If an institution wants to undertake such a venture, the starting point is deciding on the basic structure and conditions of the shared positions it will offer. Should it offer a single allotment of some or all benefits to be divided between the two faculty members? Or will each faculty member receive a full, or close to full, share of the benefits that would normally be given to a full-time faculty member? How should the tenure and promotion process be handled? Will a single tenure and promotion decision apply to both individuals sharing a position? Or will the two be evaluated separately? If the latter option is taken, what would happen if only one was granted tenure and promotion? What should the institution do if one faculty member leaves, independent of the promotion and tenure process? Offer the remaining faculty member the "whole" job? The point is merely this: it is of utmost importance that colleges and universities that decide to offer shared positions establish their basic structure and characteristics. There is no ideal structure or set of characteristics that will fit every institution. Rather, each must take into consideration its needs, its resources, and all its other particularities.
- In all cases, it is important for institutions to communicate the terms of employment to prospective faculty. Where shared positions are concerned, this is essential. Not unlike short-term, non-tenure-track positions, shared positions can take so many different forms that there is considerable room for misunderstanding. When possible, it is to the benefit of the couple sharing an appointment to have the same benefits and resources as would a single faculty member in a regular appointment. But when this is not possible, faculty must be told in advance. Likewise, full disclosure of all other features of the position is essential.

The relatively significant benefits and insignificant costs (to the institution) of shared positions make this approach especially intriguing. The keys to making such appointments work are thoughtfully working out the particulars well in advance and clearly communicating them to prospective faculty. We conclude from our case studies that shared and split positions work very well for some people. The couple's willingness to participate in this arrangement is undoubtedly another key to the success of this option for accommodating spouses and partners.

Joint Advertising of Positions

Joint advertising of positions is a way of allowing prospective candidates to know the array of openings in a specific region. No institutional contact on behalf of a candidate is necessarily involved, nor is it possible to really assess the effectiveness of this strategy, since no one may know if a spouse or partner finds a position as a result of a joint advertisement. However, aside from, perhaps, perceived competition among institutions, our research suggests that joint advertising is an important recruiting tool, particularly for small colleges. Given the large number of positions open at a large research university in any one year, sharing an advertisement with nearby institutions may be impractical. Having said this, we make the following recommendations:

- The success of this strategy is aided by good communication among the colleges involved, especially at the academic dean level. Joint advertising clearly works best when the academic deans know each other and are willing to make calls on behalf of sought-after candidates yet do not impose on their colleagues too strenuously.

Creating Tenure-Track Positions for Dual-Career Academics

For institutions considering a policy to support the creation of tenure-track positions for accompanying spouses or partners, there are some lessons to be learned from those who have already established such policies. The policy, for example, needs to be firm on the following provisions:

- The department hiring the accompanying partner or spouse must have complete buy-in and support the hire. Specifically, the faculty in the department need to feel that the person being hired is qualified for the position, meets a departmental need, and would be a good fit with the department. Even if central administration were to completely pay for a faculty line, if the department itself does not support the hire, the result will undoubtedly be negative all around. The department faculty will feel resentful, the hire will feel unwelcome, and any potential positive recruitment or retention benefit is likely to be fleeting.

- Promise nothing. No matter how comprehensive a dual-career hiring policy is, there is no way that every couple is going to be accommodated as they might like. The best an academic institution can do is to try—even if an accompanying partner does not find the position he or she is looking for. Promising someone that a partner will find a job, let alone a tenure-track position, is a mistake—especially if the institution cannot deliver on the promise. The couple is likely to experience resentment, frustration, and other negative feelings.

Variations in Accommodation Policies That Involve Creating Tenure-Track Positions

The level of institutional awareness of a dual-career hiring policy will affect how the policy is used and should be considered carefully. It is unclear whether institutions with more open policies accommodate more partners than those with less publicized ones. It is also unclear from the data which approach is better—either for the institutions or for the couples. Both approaches have their positive and negative aspects.

The Formal, Open Approach

The open approach, as taken by the University of Arizona and the University of Illinois, for example, makes all faculty candidates aware of the possibility that the university might hire a partner or spouse in a tenure-track line. Institutions that opt for this open approach to accommodation assume the onus of bringing up the issue rather than leaving it to the candidate. There seem to be several benefits to this approach. First, it can be viewed as fairer, in that all job candidates are given the opportunity to have their partners considered for dual-career hires. It can also be seen as fairer from the viewpoint of the hiring department—all department chairs and search committee heads know that the institution has the policy and thus can use it to help recruit good faculty members. Second, the open approach supports equal opportunity hiring regulations that prohibit interviewers from asking job candidates about their partner status; if the issue is brought up to all candidates, then there is no need to ask individuals if this is a concern. Third, such an approach recognizes that the attempt to accommodate a partner is a lengthy undertaking that ought to be initiated early in the search process rather than later. If an academic unit knows during the interview stage that hiring a partner is an important factor in whether a candidate will accept an offer, the institution can start exploring options earlier in the process. Fourth, having a written policy is good for public relations, both within and outside the institution, and may help to attract more scholars to the position. Many institutions with more public policies say in job advertisements that they are willing to consider the needs of dual-career couples. This might attract candidates who otherwise would not have applied. The downside of having a more open policy is that more candidates are likely to request an accommodation, which can be very time consuming and potentially costly. A related downside occurs when an accommodation is requested and the outcome is not what the couple would have liked. In such cases not only is the couple disappointed, but the other faculty members trying to make the accommodation may feel disheartened. Having a policy in writing can also create some inflexibility and could become so detailed and bureaucratic that it might discourage department chairs from pursuing an accommodation.

The Unwritten Approach

Unwritten policies tend, by definition, to be less systematic and less well publicized. The main advantage of having an unwritten policy is that it typically allows for greater flexibility. Large bureaucracies, including many institutions of higher education, can become so rule-bound that it is difficult to meet special circumstances. If dual-career accommodations are handled ad hoc, this problem is more easily avoided. The greatest disadvantage of an unwritten policy is ethical in nature. This is especially problematic in cases where the policy is both unwritten and not widely known to exist. Most observers would conclude that policies that benefit those who are aware of them, while disadvantaging those out of the loop, are simply unfair.

The Matter of Fairness

Whether a policy is written or unwritten, basic fairness requires that it govern the behavior of all equally and not advantage the privileged few. Essential to making dual-career accommodations fair is ensuring that everyone has an equal chance of benefiting from the policy. The key phrase here is "equal chance." No one would argue that every couple who requests an accommodation should receive one. The point is rather that a couple's chance for accommodation ought not to be affected by extraneous factors—in this case, whether a search committee chair was aware that an accommodation might be possible. The reality, however, is that dual-career accommodations involving tenure-track positions are typically lengthy, involved, political, and difficult to undertake. Colleges and universities simply cannot make accommodations in every case without running the risk of distorting curriculum and departmental needs and creating a backlash among the faculty. Most of the faculty and administrators at Riverdale and Hilltop believe that dual-career accommodations should be attempted only when the initial hire is of such a high caliber that the energy spent in finding work for his or her partner is likely to be worth it. Neither institution wanted to impose on other departments unless they really wanted the initial hire. At these institutions, the receiving department understood that requests for accommodation were made selectively and therefore took such requests seriously.

Sharing the Cost of a New Position

How academic departments and the central administration share the cost of hiring an accompanying spouse or partner is a variation worth considering. At question is whether the new position ought to be funded through bridge money (a temporary "loan" from to the hiring department) or as a more permanent arrangement (the Provost's Office and the department of the initial hire continue to pay two-thirds of the position of the accompanying spouse or partner). The most popular approach seems to be temporarily funding a position. The advantage of the bridge approach is that it recognizes that the department hiring the accompanying partner is responsible for taking ownership of the hire, and it might encourage department faculty to treat the person better than if the position were funded externally. The advantage of the more permanent cost-sharing approach is that it recognizes that the accompanying partner might not have been hired without some intervention and allows for more flexibility by the department hiring the accompanying partner; it can hire someone for a position even if it hadn't planned to before this opportunity arose. The permanent money shift also tells the department making the initial hire that this ought to be someone they truly value—since it will cost it a considerable amount over the long term. The department receiving the accompanying partner benefits from the long-term arrangement because it gets a full-time faculty member at one-third of the cost.

It is important to note that the cost-sharing arrangements of any particular institution are contingent on how it handles the funding of faculty lines. If, as in many cases, faculty lines are "owned" by the central administration, to be doled out to departments and schools competitively, this affects how dual-career positions are funded. If this is the case, then the priorities of the institution as a whole, for example, will be given more prominence when determining whether and how to fund a faculty line for an accompanying spouse or partner.

Creating the New Position

Who shepherds the creation of the new faculty position through the institution is another aspect that varies slightly between institutions. At most institutions with dual-career hiring policies, the department chair hiring the initial person is responsible for discussing the issues with deans, other department chairs, an equal opportunity representative, and eventually the chief academic officer. This puts a lot of responsibility on one person, which may lead to a variety of outcomes. The ability of any department chair to put together an arrangement that involves so many actors and so much politics can be difficult, and success may rest strongly on the abilities of that one person. Recognizing the limitations of such an approach, administrators at the University of California, Davis, created a central office to handle such details. This is the only case we could find of an "outside" party's taking control over the potential creation of a new position—the institution's rationale makes some sense, since it puts the obligation for a successful match not on the personalities and abilities of department heads, but in a more centralized location.

Concluding Comment

We believe it is important for academic institutions to acknowledge the growing number of academic couples vying for faculty positions. This is a trend that will continue, and for most institutions, especially those in isolated regions, it would be unwise to ignore the issue. That is not to say that every institution needs to or should implement a full-scale dual-career accommodation policy or that every dual-career couple will be accommodated as they may desire. Rather, institutions that wish to be competitive for the best faculty should at least consider their stance regarding this complex issue and decide what kind of accommodation policy they are willing to create given their own campus culture and needs. This is especially true as more and more institutions are creating such policies or are at least willing to consider ad hoc accommodations for the spouses and partners of highly desirable faculty. To be competitive, colleges and universities will need to at least keep pace with their peer institutions on this issue.

The parallel between the needs of dual-career couples searching for desirable academic positions close to one another and the two-body problem as described by physicists is striking. In physics the two-body problem is relatively easy to solve when one takes into account the "size" or "stature" of each object. Similarly, if there were only two bodies involved, the problem of dual-career couples would also be relatively simple. There is, however, a third body: the hiring institution, which further complicates the problem. As in physics, when one adds a third element to the problem—the institution and its needs—the solution becomes more elusive. In physics, the problem of exactly determining the relative motion of three bodies has not yet been solved (Wolfram 2002). We hope the information in this book brings us closer to a workable solution for dual-career couples.

APPENDIX A

Survey Methodology

This study uses survey research to assess the range of policies and practices that institutions of higher education use to address spouse or partner accommodation. We created the survey instrument to allow respondents to explain whether and how their institutions have addressed the needs of dual-career couples. Because there are no national data to outline the range of approaches that have been tried and no evidence on what types of programs, practices, or policies seem to be effective in addressing this issue, the survey is exploratory. We developed the survey after conducting hour-long interviews with three administrators at an institution that has an established dual-career policy. The survey contains both forced-choice and open-ended questions, leading to analysis of both qualitative and quantitative data. Given the lack of systematic data on this topic and the absence of an existing model to test, our analysis is necessarily inductive.

Once it was pilot-tested, we administered the survey to chief academic officers at institutions that belong to the Association of American Colleges and Universities (AAC&U). AAC&U is the only higher education association whose main aim is to improve undergraduate liberal education; its membership includes over six hundred public and private colleges and universities. AAC&U gave us permission to use its mailing list to distribute the survey. The response rate was 360 out of 617 schools, or 59 percent. For a copy of the survey, contact the authors.

APPENDIX B

Useful Internet Resources

The following are sample university policies and resources on hiring dual-career couples.

Relocation Service and Career Network Offices

Arizona State University
www.asu.edu/hr/jobs/relocation.html

Bowling Green State University
www.bgsu.edu/offices/pr/monitor/pastissues/4-27-98/guide.html

Johns Hopkins University
www.jhu.edu/ffihr1/carmgt/2career.htm

Ohio University
www.ohiou.edu/dual/

Pennsylvania State University
www.ohr.psu.edu/EMPLMNT/programs.htm#DualCareer

Purdue University
www.purdue.edu/humanrel/HTML_Files/SpousalRelocation/Programs/programs.html

Texas A&M University
hr.tamu.edu/employment/partner/pdf

University of Arkansas
hr.uark.edu/programs/DualCareerEmploymentNetwork.asp

University of California, Davis
provost.ucdavis.edu/pop/popcvr.cfm

University of California, Santa Cruz
www2.ucsc.edu/ahr/dcs/

University of Illinois at Urbana-Champaign
www.provost.uiuc.edu/provost/appointments/recruit.html

University of Iowa
www.uiowa.edu/ffiprovost/dcn/

University of Maryland
www.inform.umd.edu/EdRes/FacRes/programs/#dual

University of Michigan
www.umich.edu/%7Eprovost/programs/dualcar.html

University of Minnesota
www.umn.edu/ohr/rap

University of Nebraska, Kearney
www.unk.edu/offices/dcp/hub2.html

University of Nebraska, Lincoln
www.unl.edu/svcaa/faculty/dualcareer.html

University of Nebraska, Omaha
www.unomaha.edu/aa/dual%20career%20statement.htm

Policies on Shared and Split Positions

Grinnell Collegeweb.grinnell.edu/Dean/Forms/shared-pos.htm
www.grinnell.edu/offices/dean/chairinfo/sharedpos/
hven.swarthmore.edu/ffijensen/grinnell_policy.html

Policies related to the Appointment of a Spouse or Partner to an Academic Position

Arizona State University, College of Liberal Arts and Sciences hven.
swarthmore.edu/ffijensen/asu_partner.html

Indiana University–Purdue University Fort Wayne
www.ipfw.edu/vcaa/Fac_Info/searchwaiver.pdf

Kansas State University
www.ksu.edu/ddcd/

Texas A&M University
hr.tamu.edu/employment/partner.pdf

University of Arizona
www.arizona.edu/ffivprovacf/couples/guidelines.htm

University of Michigan
www.umich.edu/%7Eprovost/programs/dualcar.html

Western Washington University
www.ac.wwu.edu/ffisenate/senate/handbook/appdixk.html

Nepotism Policies

Arizona State University
www.asu.edu/aad/manuals/spp/spp205.html

Central Michigan University
www.hrs.cmich.edu/spg-nepotism.htm

Howard University
www.hr.howard.edu/hrm/policy/Nepotism%20Policy.htm

Tulane University
www.tmc.tulane.edu/researchadmin/NepotismPolicy.html

University of Iowa
www.uiowa.edu/ffiour/opmanual/iii/08.htm

Comprehensive Policy Statements on Partner Accommodation

Michigan State University
www.msu.edu/unit/facrecds/proced/ahms09.html

Northern Arizona University
www.nau.edu/ffiaffirm/forms/partner.html

University of Colorado System
www.cu.edu/ffipolicies/Personnel/dual.html

University of North Carolina
www.unc.edu/faculty/faccoun/reports/R97FWC1.htm

University of Wisconsin
www.wisc.edu/provost/hiring/spousal.html

BIBLIOGRAPHY

Aebersold, N. 2001. *Dual career service 2000–2001: Summary of accomplishments and survey results*. Santa Cruz: University of California.

Aisenberg, N., and Harrington, M. 1988. *Women of academe: Outsiders in the sacred grove*. Amherst: University of Massachusetts Press.

American Association of University Professors. 1966. Statement on Government of Colleges and Universities. www.aaup.org/statements/Redbook/Govern.htm. Retrieval date 3/18/03.

———. 2001. Statement of principles on family responsibilities and academic work. www.aaup.org/statements/REPORTS/reo1fam.htm. Retrieval date 3/18/03.

Association of Governing Boards of Colleges and Universities. 1995. *Ten public policy issues for higher education in 1995*. AGB public policy series 95–1. Washington, DC: AGB.

Astin, H. S., and D. E. Davis. 1985. Research productivity across the life and career cycles: Facilitators and barriers for women. In *Scholarly writing and publishing: Issues, problems, and solutions*, ed. M. F. Fox. Boulder, CO: Westview Press.

Astin, H. S., and J. F. Milem. 1997. The status of academic couples in U.S. institutions. In *Academic couples: Problems and promises*, ed. M. A. Ferber and J. W. Loeb. Urbana: University of Illinois Press.

Baldwin, R., and J. Chronister. 2001. *Teaching without tenure: Policies and practices for a new era*. Baltimore: Johns Hopkins University Press.

Bellas, M. L. 1992. The effects of marital status and wives' employment on the salaries of faculty men: The (house) wife bonus. *Gender and Society* 6 (4): 609–22.

———. 1997. The scholarly productivity of academic couples. In *Academic couples: Problems and promises*, ed. M. A. Ferber and J. W. Loeb. Urbana: University of Illinois Press.

Bellas, M. L., and R. K. Toutkoushian 1999. Faculty time allocations and research productivity: Gender, race, and family effects. *Review of Higher Education* 22:367–90.

Berger, M., M. Foster, B. S. Wallston, and L. Wright. 1977. You and me against the world: Dual career couples and joint job seeking. *Journal of Research and Development in Education* 10 (4): 30–37.

Bird, G. W., and G. A. Bird. 1987. In pursuit of academic careers: Observations and reflections of a dual-career couple. *Family Relations* 36:97–100.

Birnbaum, R. 1983. *Maintaining institutional diversity in higher education.* San Francisco: Jossey-Bass.

Boice, R. 1992. *The new faculty member: Supporting and fostering professional development.* San Francisco: Jossey-Bass.

Bond, T., E. Galinsky, and J. Swanberg. 1998. *The 1997 national study of the changing workforce.* New York: Families and Work Institute.

Bowen, H., and J. Schuster. 1986. *American professors: A national resource imperiled.* New York: Oxford University Press.

Bowen, W. G., and J. A. Sosa. 1989. *Prospects for faculty in the arts and sciences.* Princeton: Princeton University Press.

Bruce, W. 1990. Dual career couples in the university: Policies and problems. Paper presented at the Annual Conference of the National Association for Women Deans, Administrators and Counselors, Nashville, TN.

Burke, D. 1988. *A new academic marketplace.* New York: Greenwood Press.

Caplow, T., and R. J. McGee. 1958. *The academic marketplace.* New York: Basic Books.

Carroll, L. 1930. *Through the looking-glass.* New York: Macmillan.

Center for Work and Family Balance. 2002. Composition of working households, 1920–2000. www.workandfamily.org/xls/table15WorkingHouseholds.xls. Retrieval date 3/18/03.

Clark, S. M., and M. Corcoran. 1986. Perspectives on the professional socialization of women faculty: A case of accumulative disadvantage. *Journal of Higher Education* 57 (1): 20–43.

Costa, D. L, and M. E. Kahn. 1999. Power couples: Changes in the locational choice of the college educated, 1940–1990. NBER Working Paper 7109. nber.org/papers/W7109. Retrieval date 3/18/03.

Creamer, E. G. 2001. *Working equal: Academic couples as collaborators.* New York: Routledge Falmer.

Department of Defense. 1988. Directive 1400.33. usmilitary.about.com/library/mil-info/dodreg/bldodreg1400–33.htm. Retrieval date 3/18/03.

Dewey, J. 1916. *Democracy and education: An introduction to the philosophy of education.* New York: Macmillan.

Didion, C. J. 1996. Dual careers and shared positions: Adjusting university policy to accommodate academic couples. *Journal of College Science Teaching* 26 (2): 123–24.

Eby, L. T., and T. D. Allen. 1998. Perceptions of relocation services in relocation decision making: An exploratory field study. *Group and Organization Management* 23 (4): 447.

Ferber, M. A., and J. W. Loeb. 1997. *Academic couples: Problems and promises.* Urbana: University of Illinois Press.

Finkelstein, M. J. 1984. *The American academic profession: A synthesis of social scientific inquiry since World War II.* Columbus: Ohio State University Press.

Finkelstein, M. J., R. K. Seal, and J. H. Schuster. 1998. *The new academic generation: A profession in transformation.* Baltimore: Johns Hopkins University Press.

Gappa, J. M. 1987. The stress-producing working conditions of part-time faculty. *New Directions for Teaching and Learning, Coping with Faculty Stress* 29:33–42.

Gee, E. G. 1991. The dual-career couple: A growing challenge. *Educational Record* 72: 45–47.

Grant, L., I. Kennelly, and K. B. Ward. 2000. Revisiting the gender, marriage, and parenthood puzzle in scientific careers. *Women's Studies Quarterly* 1–2:62–85.

Hendershott, A. 1995. A moving story for spouses and other wage-earners: Husbands who relocate because of their wives' jobs. *Psychology Today* 28 (5): 28–31.

Hensel, N. 1991. *Realizing gender equality in higher education: The need to integrate work/family issues.* ASHE-ERIC Higher Education Report 2. Washington, DC: George Washington University School of Education and Human Development.

Hogan, C. 1998. Dual career couple hiring at baccalaureate I colleges. Paper presented at the annual meeting of the Association for the Study of Higher Education, Sacramento, CA.

Innis-Dagg, A. 1993. Academic faculty wives and systemic discrimination—anti-nepotism and "inbreeding." *Canadian Journal of Higher Education* 23 (1): 1–18.

Jarvis, D. K. 1992. Improving junior faculty scholarship. In *Developing new and junior faculty*, ed. M. D. Sorcinelli and A. E. Austin, 63–72. San Francisco: Jossey-Bass.

Katterman, L. 1995. Splitting faculty positions allows couples to integrate research and family. *Scientist* 9 (21): 16–17.

Lambda Legal Defense and Education Fund. 1992. Domestic partnership: Issues and legislation. New York: Lambda Legal Defense and Education Fund.

Lewis, L. S. 1975. *Scaling the ivory tower: Merit and its limits in academic careers.* Baltimore: Johns Hopkins University Press.

Lincoln, Y. S., and Guba, E. G. 1985. *Naturalistic inquiry.* Beverly Hills, CA: Sage.

Loeb, J. W. 1997. Programs for academic partners: How well can they work? In *Academic couples: Problems and promises*, ed. M. A. Ferber and J. W. Loeb. Urbana: University of Illinois Press.

Long, J. S. 1990. The origins of sex differences in science. *Social Forces* 71:159–78.

Lucas, C. 1998. Moving out, moving in: The army's pilot program in outsourcing relocation. Mobility, www.cendantmobility.com/cendant/pub_articles/army_pilot.html. Retrieval date 3/18/03.

Martin, R. 1999. Adjusting to job relocation: Relocation preparation can reduce relocation stress. *Journal of Occupational and Organizational Psychology* 72 (2): 231–36.

McElrath, K. 1992. Gender, career disruption, and academic rewards. *Journal of Higher Education* 63 (3): 270–81.

McLoud, P. 2001. hr.uark.edu/programs/DualCareerEmploymentNetwork.asp. Retrieval date 3/18/03.

McNeil, L., and Sher, M. 1998. Report on the dual career couple survey. www.physics.wm.edu/ffisher/survey.html.

Merton, R. K. 1988. The Matthew effect in science, II: Cumulative advantage and symbolism of intellectual property. *Isis* 79 (229): 606–23.

Miller-Loessi, K., and D. Henderson. 1997. Changes in American society: The context for academic couples. In *Academic couples: Problems and promises*, ed. M. A. Ferber and J. W. Loeb. Urbana: University of Illinois Press.

Moen, P., D. Harris-Abbott, S. Lee, and P. Roehling. 1999. *The Cornell couples and careers study*. Ithaca, NY: Cornell Employment and Family Careers Institute, Cornell University.

Monk-Turner, E., and C. G. Turner. 1986. Dual career academic couples: Analysis of problems and a proposal for change. *Women and Politics* 6 (3): 43–55.

National Center for Education Statistics. 2002. *Digest of education statistics, 2001*. Washington DC: NCES.

Nidiffer, J. 2001. Advocates on campus: Deans of women create a new profession. In *Women administrators in higher education: Historical and contemporary perspectives*, ed. J. Nidiffer and C. T. Bashaw, 135–56. Albany: SUNY Press.

Norrell, J. E., and T. H. Norrell, 1996. Faculty and family policies in higher education. *Journal of Family Issues* 17 (2): 204–26.

Organization Resources Counselors, Inc. 1998. Trends in international assignments. www.relojournal.com/jan98/orc.htm. Retrieval date 3/18/03.

Palmieri, P. A. 1995. *In Adamless Eden: The community of women faculty at Wellesley*. New Haven: Yale University Press.

Patton, M. Q. 1990. *Qualitative evaluation and research methods*. Newbury Park, CA: Sage.

Perkins, L. 1997. For the good of the race: Married African-American academics—a historical perspective. In *Academic couples: Problems and promises*, ed. M. A. Ferber and J. W. Loeb. Urbana: University of Illinois Press.

Preissler, S. M. 1989. Job search help for the "trailing spouse." *Journal of Career Planning and Employment* 50:83–84.

Raabe, P. H. 1997. Work-family policies for faculty: How "career-and family-friendly" is academe? In *Academic couples: Problems and promises*, ed. M. A. Ferber and J. W. Loeb. Urbana: University of Illinois Press.

Rathert, C. 2001. Participant responses to spousal employment assistance program. Paper presented at the Midwest Academy of Management, Toledo, OH, April 19.

Reed, C., and W. Bruce. 1993. Dual career couples in the public sector: A survey of personnel policies and practices. *Public Personnel Management* 22 (2): 187–99.

Rossiter, M. 1982. *Women scientists in America: Struggles and Strategies to 1940*. Baltimore: Johns Hopkins University Press.

Schneider, A. 1998. Recruiting academic stars: New tactics in an old game. *Chronicle of Higher Education*, May 29. A2.

Shoben, E. W. 1997. From anti-nepotism rules to programs for partners: Legal issues. In *Academic couples: Problems and promises*, ed. M. A. Ferber and J. W. Loeb. Urbana: University of Illinois Press.

Smart, M. S., and R. C. Smart. 1990. Paired prospects: Dual-career couples on campus. *Academe* 76:33–37.

Smith, D., Wolf-Wendel, L. E., Busenberg, B., and associates. 1996. *Achieving faculty diversity: Debunking the myths.* Washington, DC: American Association of Colleges and Universities.

Sorcinelli, M. D., and J. P. Near. 1989. Relations between work and life away from work among university faculty. *Journal of Higher Education* 60 (1): 59–82.

Stafford, S. G., and G. B. Spanier. 1990. Recruiting the dual career couple: The family employment program. *Initiatives* 53 (2): 37–44.

Strauss, A., and J. Corbin. 1990. *Basics of qualitative research: Grounded theory procedures and techniques.* Newbury Park, CA: Sage.

Thaller, M. February 25, 2002. A romance written in the stars.www.csmonitor.com/ atcsmonitor/cybercoverage/thaller/p-5170ithallerdual.html.

Uhland, V. 1999. If Mama's not happy. *Denver Rocky Mountain News*, July 25.

Ward, K. B., and Grant, L. 1996. Gender and academic publishing. In *Higher education: Handbook of theory and research*, ed. J. C. Smart, 11:172–212. New York: Agathon.

Williams, J. 1999. *Unbending gender: Why work and family conflict and what to do about it.* New York: Oxford University Press.

Wilson, R. 1996a. Faculty couples face a tight job market. *Chronicle of Higher Education*, September 20, A10–11.

———. 1996b. A report praises 29 colleges for "family friendly" policies. *Chronicle of Higher Education*, October 11, A13–15.

———. 1998. When office mates are also roommates. *Chronicle of Higher Education*, April 17, A2.

———. 1999. The frustrating career of the trailing spouse. *Chronicle of Higher Education*, March 19, A2.

———. 2001. The backlash against hiring couples. *Chronicle of Higher Education*, April 13, A2.

Windham/NFTC 1995. Multinational employers for working spouses handbook, Global relocation trends survey. www.house.gov/lofgren/dc/mews.html. Retrieval date 8/9/02.

Wolfram, S. 2002. *A new kind of science.* Champaign, IL: Wolfram Media.

Wolf-Wendel, L. E., S. Twombly, and S. Rice. 2000. Dual-career couples: Keeping them together. *Journal of Higher Education* 71 (3): 291–321.

INDEX